APPLIED LINGUISTICS

A GENRE ANALYSIS OF:
Research Articles Results and Discussion
Sections in Journals Published
in Applied Linguistics

Veronica M. Mutinda

authorHOUSE®

AuthorHouse™
1663 Liberty Drive
Bloomington, IN 47403
www.authorhouse.com
Phone: 1 (800) 839-8640

Published by AuthorHouse 12/15/2017

ISBN: 978-1-5462-1999-6 (sc)
ISBN: 978-1-5462-1998-9 (e)

Library of Congress Control Number: 2017918643

Contents

CHAPTER ONE

CHAPTER TWO

CHAPTER THREE

CHAPTER FOUR

CHAPTER FIVE

List of Tables

List of Figures

Operational Definition of Terms

Communicative purposes: The function(s) of a section of the Research Articles i.e. what the author is doing in each section.

Discourse community: A local and temporary constraining system, defined by a body of texts (or more generally practices) that are unified by a common focus. It is a textual system with stated and unstated conventions. In our study the area of writing research articles in journals of Applied Linguistics makes up a discourse community.

Genre: A class of recognizable communicative events and that shares communication purposes and modes.

Genre analysis: the study of how language is used to organize genre into patterns. It helps us understand how language is used within a discourse community i.e. the rules and conventions governing a discourse community.

Move: the rhetorical division/unit of a text that has different and unique communicative purpose(s) that reflect the writer's purpose and the conventions laid down by the discourse community.

Obligatory Move: a move that occurs at a high frequency and found in all the research article studied.

Optional Move: a move that occurs at a very low frequency and does not occur in all the research article sections studied.

Rhetorical structure: the order of the moves in a text or a segment of a text such as the Results and Conclusion sections of a Research Article in this study.

Step: A rhetorical division of the move that carries a communicative purpose. Also called the 'element.'

V + ing phrases: Verb phrases used by the author to reflect the intended communicative purpose such as reporting results, commenting on results, summarizing results etc.

List of Acronyms

CARS   - Create a Research Space
DM   - Discussion Move
EAP   - English for Academic Purposes
ESP   - English for Specific Purposes
IMRD   - Introduction, Methods, Results and
            Discussion
MA   - Master of Arts
MSc   - Master of Science
RA   - Research Article
RAI   - Research Article Introduction
RD   - Results and Discussions
RM   - Results Move
DM   - Discussions Move
Vol.   - Volume

Dedication

For Jay, Frida, Felicia and Fabian

For your prayers, love, support,
understanding and patience.

Preface

In this book, I have dealt with genre analysis of research article (RA) Results and Discussion sections in journals published in Applied Linguistics. The research articles are related to English language education. To come up with the book, I investigated the Rhetorical Structure and described the rhetorical functions of the aforementioned research article sections. I also investigated if there are any differences and/or similarities between the rhetorical structures of the results and discussion sections of research articles in journals published in Applied Linguistics. To do this I was guided by Swales' (1990, 2004), Yang & Allison (2003) and Kanoksilapatham (2007) move structure models to study the results section. As for the discussion section I was guided by Swales' (1990), Yang & Allison (2003) and Rasmeenin (2006) move models. I employed situated qualitative research design to purposively select ten (10) research articles each from ten journals selected through non-probability sampling methods. These were journals published in Applied Linguistics in the year 2013. I used Genre Theory to guide the exercise of analyzing the data. My aim is to provide insight in the field of Applied Linguistics and particularly in genre analysis of academic texts. As illustrated in the book,

I found that the rhetorical structure of both Results and Discussions sections were similar in terms of the number of moves found but noted difference in terms of the focus of each section. Both sections have six moves and the focus of the results section is to report results whereas the discussion section in a RA serves to explain the results. My goal for this book is to provide knowledge to my audience or readers that not only assists upcoming academicians to fit in their specific discourse communities, but also help in teaching of research article writing. The importance and place of this book as a great resource to help learners understand the process of effective communication and organization of ideas in writing the genre I have discussed here can never be over- emphasized.

CHAPTER ONE
Introduction

This chapter includes the background information of the subject of this book. Traditionally, describing the rules of English usage; that is, grammar, is one of the aims of linguistics. Widdowson (1978), however, notes that recent studies have moved their focus and attention from merely giving a definition of the standard features of language usage to exploring the ways in which language is actually used in day to day communication. He also reports that the language we speak and write varies in different ways from one context to another due to the conventions of each context also known as discourse community. This makes it possible to establish the features of particular situations and contexts then use these features to teach learners how to function in these situations.

Situation refers to discourse community. Widdowson (1978) and Duszak (1997) argue that the English required by a particular discourse community could be identified by studying the linguistic characteristics noted in their area of work or study. Berkenkotter and Huckin (1993), Miller (1984) and Connor (1994) say that genre is shaped by the author's knowledge of the audience or whom (the discourse community) a genre is intended. Swales and Feak (1994, 2004) note that many factors come to play in the production of genre and these include:

-purpose, organization, presentation, and audience. Paltridge (2001) confirms this when he discusses the idea of context and audience as two very important factors influencing genre formation. Berkenkotter and Huckin (1993), Paltridge (2001) and Briones (2012) concur that genres vary a lot owing to factors such as discourse community contexts, across culture, language and field of study.

The concern of recent studies has been, therefore, to identify the patterns guiding text organization and to specify the linguistic means by which these patterns are communicated. The results of such studies have been used to establish rhetorical patterns of text organization that enhance effective and efficient as well as adequate functioning of the learners in their particular discourse community. This has motivated researchers in Applied Linguistics to focus their attention on studies aimed at informing on needs analysis and syllabus design, (Sinclair, 1986, Hyons, 1996).

Holmes (1997) notes that genre-oriented studies have recorded increasing interest and attention from academicians in the last three decades. This increasing attention is even more on the written academic genres. He attributes this increase to the need for the provision of satisfactory models and description of literary texts and the need to enable L2 speakers/learners to understand and produce their own works in the different genres they are involved in.

The field of genre analysis has seen a great number of studies on the written academic genres. Those dealing with the research article (henceforth, RA) have investigated discourse structure of the various sections in this genre such as the Introduction section (Swales 1981, 2004; Holmes 1995, Jogthong 2001, Waseema 2006, Habibi 2008 and Lakic 2010), Discussion section (Hopkins and Dudley-Evans 1988; Yang and Desmond 2002, and Rasmeenin 2006,) and the Results section (Swales and Feak 1994, Yang and Desmond 2001, 2004, Swales 2004 and Kanoksilapatham 2007) as well as the patterns of how linguistic features are used (Samraj, 2002).

Of the great number of studies carried out to date on the RA, whether on the particular sections or its overall structure, many have been focused on natural sciences. Holmes (1997) observes that a large number of L2 speaker learners are undertaking studies in social science subjects and that the medium of instruction is English. This, therefore, justifies the pedagogical rationale for extending the analysis of the RA genre into the social sciences.

The Results and subsequent sections are very important and related stages of RAs where the authors present and interpret their findings to the readers in order to establish their importance. Accordingly, I have investigated some of the means by which empirical RAs from selected journals in Applied Linguistics proceed from presenting Results and then proceed to discuss the results; described the rhetorical functions of the two sections as well as identified the similarities and differences that exist between the rhetorical structures of the Results and the Conclusions sections. To do this, I have used V(erb) + ing phrases since my focus is to establish what the RA authors are trying to do with the discourse, for example, reporting results or comparing results with literature review. This is to say that I have studied the meaning that the authors attached to discourse in order to report results, comment on results, as well as to draw conclusions from the finding of their study.

The basic understanding of the concept of genre, as now used in Applied Linguistics, English for Specific Purposes (henceforth ESP) and rhetoric, is an emphasis on the importance of the communicative purpose and the varied ways in which the need to communicate shapes or influences and determine both surface forms and deeper rhetorical structures.

The Results and Conclusions sections of the RA seem to have either been neglected or been assumed to be easy and straightforward to researchers to write, read and understand, although this is not the case as reported by Thompson (1993). Swales (1990, 2004) and Dudley-Evans (1999) note that research writing has not been given adequate attention. Genre-centered analysts avoid tackling the aspects of organizational patterns of RA sections and most studies have only dealt with parts of the RA. To date it has been noted that studies done seem to analyze each RA section as an independent entity, with the exception of the study done by Berkenkotter and Huckins (1995) which relates their analysis of the Discussion section to the Introduction section. This creates a need to investigate the rhetorical structure of the results and discussion sections of RAs in Applied Linguistics and related the results sections to the discussion section in terms of similarities and differences in the rhetorical structure and communicative focus.

Genre linguists have studied the Results and Conclusion sections of the RA but they do not seem to agree on the rhetorical structure of the said sections. There are those that give three moves and others that give six moves. This necessitated my contribution towards lessening this controversy. To accomplish this, I have to address the following:

1. describe the rhetorical structures of the Results and Conclusions sections of a Research Article.
2. describe the rhetorical functions of the Results and Conclusions sections of a Research Article.
3. compare and contrast the rhetorical structures of the Results and Conclusions sections of a Research Article.

The following questions aided me to achieve the goal of accomplishing the aforementioned tasks.

1. What are the rhetorical structures of the Results and the Conclusions sections of the Research Article?
2. What are the rhetorical functions of the Results and the Conclusions sections of the Research Article?
3. What similarities and differences exist between the rhetorical structures of the Results and Conclusions sections of a Research Article?

I set off with some assumptions to guide me towards achieving the set goals:

1. The Results and the Conclusions sections of a Research Article have unique rhetorical structures.

2. The Results and the Conclusions sections of a Research Article serve unique functions in the organization and writing of a Research Article.
3. Similarities and differences do exist between the rhetorical structures of the Results and Conclusions sections of the Research Article.

My rationale is that; English has risen to gain the status of an international language and especially in the field of academics, science and technology, (Grabe & Kaplan, 1996; Johns & Dudley-Evans, 1991). Kanoksilapatham (2005) notes that due to this status, the Research Article in English has become a main channel for advancing research knowledge among scholars world-wide. She also reports that with globalization, the ability to read and/or write RAs in English is very important for success both academically and professionally. To enable the researchers, both native and non-native speakers of English, to read and/or write a RA, there is need to be informed about the conventional rhetorical structure used in their fields of study; I concur to refer to this as the discourse community, (Paltridge, 2001; Swales & Feak 2004).

As the number of students taking graduate-level courses continue to grow, they have at one time to write a research paper or RA in their respective discourse communities. Therefore, a book like this one presenting the rhetorical structure of current RAs provides an insight in the field of Applied Linguistics and particularly in Genre Analysis of academic texts contribute in helping the upcoming academicians in writing papers that will be acceptable to their specific discourse communities.

It also provides information that can help in the structuring and interpretation of a RA, so as to provide a model and framework that can be of great help in effectiveness when applied in academic writing instruction, especially in the field of Applied Linguistics. Knowledge of how Results and Conclusions sections are developed could be a useful contribution not only in the teaching of RA writing but also in illuminating the process of effective communication and organization of thoughts in the writing of RAs.

Most of the genre studies on academic writing have dealt with the natural sciences but few have looked at humanities and social sciences and especially the Results and Discussion sections (Belanger, 1982; Dudley-Evans, 1986; Hopkins and Dudley-Evans, 1988; Brett, 1994; Holmes, 1997; Williams, 1999; Peacock, 2002; Yang and Allison, 2003; and Bunton, 2005). In view of this there is, therefore, a pedagogical rationale for extending the genre analysis of the RA and in particular the study of the particular RA sections to the social sciences. The analysis of the Results to Conclusions sections enables the researchers to establish that the organizational patterns in these sections in RAs in Applied Linguistics are applicable to other such sections of RAs in all written academic discourse.

Additionally, it provides a basic framework for the production of academic discourses in Applied Linguistics which may be of great help to readers who find it difficult to understand RAs as well as novice writers who require a better understanding of the RA genre when writing for academic and/or publication to better meet the set international academic community's conventions.

However, human beings are finite and as such all find some limitations to their work and efforts. As such, there are studies that have investigated different academic texts such as the science report Bazerman, (1988)]; the dissertation [Dudley-Evans (1999)]; the research proposal [Maroko, (1999, 2008)]; television broadcast discussion programs [Karanja, (1993)]. However, I have extended the scope by focusing on RAs and particularly the Results and Conclusion sections of RAs of journals in Applied Linguistics.

RAs consist of different parts namely: Introduction, Methods, Results and Discussion, what Swales (1990), calls IMRD. However, here I have only investigated the rhetorical structure of the last two parts – the RD. This is because analyzing a whole lengthy RA tends to result in failure to study significant details. This also approach allows one to remain within the boundaries of the selected theoretical framework.

Academic writing studies fall under two levels: those that study the process and those that focus on the product. I have focused on the product. The stages at the level of writing as a product as given by Richards (1990) include: form, discourse organization, paragraph structure, use of cohesive devices and choice of vocabulary and grammar. He further says that it is in the product of writing that the textual features of the finished items such as rhetoric, cohesive devices and text organizational patterns are evident (Richards, 1990:106-107). Taking this line of argument, I have here analyzed the rhetorical move structure of the Results and Conclusions sections of ten RAs from ten leading journals in Applied Linguistics.

There are ten (10) RAs for the corpus. Bazerman, (1988) and Lovejoy, (1991) argue that for purposes of genre studies three articles are enough for analysis. It is also argued that in genre studies even a small sample size is enough as it typifies the aspect studied across the board, (Swales, 1981, 1990; Maroko, 1999, 2008; Nyongesa, 2005). This is because genre analysis calls for finer details of the aspect studied. As such, I believe and illustrate that the number of RAs selected here are enough to give results that can be generalizable across the genre.

Conclusion

This chapter provides a background of the book and states its importance in the field of Applied Linguistics because the research article results and discussion sections have not been extensively studied. It also serves to point out that these two sections of the RA (that is the Results and Discussion sections) are very important in any research work as they report and interpret the findings of the study carried out.

CHAPTER TWO

Reviewing Related Literature and Theoretical Framework

Introduction

This chapter provides a historical background and approaches to text analysis with an aim to place this work in the context of genre studies. It also discusses the basic concepts used in the reviewing the genre studies related to Results and Conclusion sections of a RA, and discusses the theoretical framework and the tenets that guide such research. It includes:

- Approaches to Text Analysis

This subsection has information on the development of text linguistics and the different approaches used in analyzing texts. This puts the work into context by providing background information on text analysis. This subsection also endeavors to provide an overview of genre studies done in the field.

-Historical perspective and approaches to text linguistics

Nyongesa (2005) reports that linguists are concerned with finding out how human beings communicate using both spoken and written language. He adds that linguists analyze language to find out how writers structure linguistic ideas for readers and how the readers work on these ideas in an effort to interpret them. Linguistics has two main approaches to deal with the communication and interpretation of messages. These two are: discourse analysis and text analysis. Discourse analysis deals with the structure of naturally occurring data as found in speeches, interviews, conversations and debates while text analysis studies the structure of naturally occurring written language in texts like letters, essays, reports, passages, notices, stories, books and research articles.

The study of discourse and texts has faced a lot of controversy. Beaugrande (1985) argues that these two fields of study have sometimes been considered identical, sometimes opposed and even unrelated. They are said to be identical because they both originate from rhetoric and involve the study of language, above the sentence, in its context. Edmondson (1981) agrees that the terms can and are often used interchangeably. However, the distinction between the two concepts is still not very clear. Nyongesa (2005) says that the two concepts can be used to study both spoken and written language structures that have a communicative function. As such this book presents a study of the structure of written texts (Results and Conclusion sections of RAs).

Text analysis is associated with the 1920's Prague School of Linguistics. It was initiated by Vilem Mathiesius and later on in the 1960s Jan Frantisek Dane took it up and developed it further. Connor (1994) says that the Prague School of Linguistics brought the idea of Theme and Rheme to the field of text analysis. These two ideas explain how information in sentences is constructed to bring coherence in a text. Stubbs (1995), reports that the concept of text analysis was introduced to linguistics by British linguists in the 1930s. He says the British Linguists' school of thought on the concept of text analysis puts emphasis on the study of how language is used in both written and spoken contexts.

Connor (1994) reports about systemic linguistics, an approach related to text analysis which started in the 1960s with one of its proponents being Halliday. This approach stresses on the importance of analyzing the content-bearing texts and on studying the personal choices that people make when using language to communicate at a personal level (Halliday & Hasan, 1976). Studies on text and discourse analysis became very popular in the 1980s.

Studies in this approach of text analysis are done at two levels. First there are those studies at macro-level text structure that study a text by looking at its lexis and grammar. Here sample studies include those by Halliday & Hasan (1976) on Cohesion in the English language in general and Halliday (1985) who analyzed the interplay that exists between a language and the functions that the language serves in social settings. Secondly, we have studies based at micro-level text structure. Studies at this level aim at providing an analysis of the rhetorical structure of various texts such as the RAs.

This level includes the works of Swales (1990) on the structure of RA introductions; Salager-Meyer on hedging and discourse in RAs (1992); Bolivar (1994) who analyzed English newspapers editorials; Ogutu (1996), and Onguko (1999) on cohesion and coherence in written texts and Maroko (1999) on the rhetorical structure of Masters of Arts research proposals. Just like the cited studies, I have here investigated the rhetorical structure of the Results and Conclusion sections) of RAs at micro-structure level.

- Genre Analysis Studies

Some genre linguists have investigated different aspects of genre writing such as cohesion and coherence (Ogutu 1996, Karanja 1993, Onguko 1999) and the rhetorical structure, Maroko (1999, 2008), and Nyongesa (2005).

Ogutu (1996) analyses cohesion and coherence structure on texts written by secondary school English as second language learners. In her study she attempts to quantify coherence and to show its levels in various texts through evidence of cohesive markers present. She says that cohesion upholds the hanging together of a text, especially through a chain interaction of cohesive features.

Karanja (1993) identifies the linguistic resources available to second language English users in maintaining discussions in her study on how clarity, cohesion and coherence are achieved in Kenya Broadcasting Corporation Television discussion programs. She says that these discussions are found to be too rigid and, thus, unnatural due to too much censorship during production.

A comparative study of cohesion in academic and newspaper texts was carried out by Onguko (1999). She studied how static and dynamic cohesive ties contribute to the overall coherence of road traffic accident reports from newspaper articles and excerpts of written academic texts. She also investigated the devices that contribute significantly to the unity of the text and hence a text's overall communicative effect. She points out that the authors of both academic and newspaper texts require to use static and dynamic cohesive ties in order to come up with texts that are cohesive enough for the reader to understand.

Nyongesa (2005) studied the rhetorical structure of the editorial sections of two Kenyan newspapers; the Daily Nation and The Standard. He studied how the structure of these two sections are developed and argues that this knowledge is a useful contribution in the teaching and of writing newspaper editorials and also in illuminating the process of effective communication of ideas to persuade or convince the readers. He notes that the rhetorical rules of specialized areas of use need to be learned by prospective writers so that they may know the semantic structure of sentences to use. He further points out that the choice of sentence semantic structure in turn determines the grammatical choices that the writer should make to communicate effectively.

In his study of the typology and ideology in the Kenyan newspaper discourse, from a critical Discourse Analysis, Mbugua (1997) observes that editorials have an organized structure. He adds that all the structural parts are equally important and have a few typographical features that guide the readers through the text.

Maroko (2008) carried out a genre analysis of Masters of Arts (MA) and Masters of Science (MSc) theses of Kenyan public universities. He uncovers the communicative purposes used, describes how writers use generic features such as moves, tense, citation and authorial stance and hedging to realize the typical communicative purposes. He reveals that the notion of communicative purposes is 'very versatile as the different levels of the thesis express diverse purpose' (Maroko 2008: ix).

This review of genre studies reflects a gap that calls for research especially on the RA. It points to an argument that the RA in Applied Linguistics has been understudied.

-Basic Concepts

Under this sub-section the idea of genre and genre analysis, and Moves will feature prominently. An elaboration of these ideas to place them in the context is therefore provided in this subsection.

-Genre and genre analysis

Genre analysis is an area of study that falls under the broad field of study; English for Specific Purposes (ESP) which is a very important mode of text analysis. This term was first used in relation to the ESP field by Swales (1991) who says that this is a mode of analysis that aims to unveil the structure of organization of a genre and the language employed by the author to bring out this organizational structure.

Genre analysis has received a lot of interest from linguists in the last three decades. This field owes its interest to the fact that it provides a framework for analyzing the communicative functions found in a genre and for identifying the linguistic patterns of the analyzed functions. Thus, it influences the teaching and learning of ESP. Flowerdew (2002) says that genre analysis is an area of study which uses functional grammar theories to analyze the realization of communicative functions and their organization into a structure that defines a genre.

Long and Richards (1995) point out that; genre analysis enhances our understanding of the usage of language in a situation. These two linguists also add that by use of both linguistic and sociolinguistic theories, genre analysis helps us to analyze how language is learned and used in an educational setting.

A general definition of genre explains that a genre is a text the members of a given discourse community recognize and label as such. The members have to agree to the stylistic and linguistic features which make up the given genre to enable it fulfill the expected communicative functions.

Swales provides a more specific definition of genre:

> *"A genre comprises a class of communicative events, the members of which serve some set of communicative purposes. These purposes are recognized by the expert members of the parent discourse community, and thereby constitute the rationale for the genre. This rationale shapes the schematic structure of the*

discourse and influences and constrains choice
of content and style," (Swales 1990:58).

Genre analysis is not exclusively focused on classifying genre but also deals with describing the structural framework of the communicative purpose and linguistic features in texts on genres. This knowledge helps in the development of ESP materials and curriculum for writing and teaching. A review of several earlier studies (notably, Dudley-Evans, 1986; Hopkins and Dudley-Evans, 1988; Bhatia 1993; Swales, 2004; and Samraj, 2002) points to a conclusion that the interest by academicians on genre studies has increased.

Maroko, (2008:13) notes that:

"Genre has recently become a popular framework for analyzing the form and rhetorical functions of non-literary discourse such as research articles, theses/dissertations, textbooks and editorials."

He further argues that genre serves as a tool that helps develop educational practices in the areas of rhetoric, composition studies, linguistics, English for Specific Purposes (ESP) and English for Academic Purposes (EAP). The reason for the increased interest is the need to provide comprehensive materials and curriculum that can be easily adopted as a teaching and learning tool by upcoming writers to communicate effectively and efficiently.

Swales (1990), sees genre analysis as an approach that enables teachers to understand the rhetorical organization of texts and that helps prepare students for writing or reading primary texts in their discourse communities. A genre, therefore, is seen as a complete text (Swales, 1990). Genres thus, gives samples on how to develop a text and genre analysis principally talks more of common features among genres belonging to the same discourse community rather than claim that genres have fixed characteristics in terms of form and style thus leading the study to conclude that those genres that do not conform to the set form and style do not belong.

Ensuing from I therefore, set out to study the RA so as to describe the rhetorical structure of its Results and Conclusions sections, the communicative purposes of the said sections, the similarities and differences, if any, in the communicative purposes and the linguistic signaling of the sections under study. The goal is to provide pedagogic help to teachers on the teaching of academic writing within EAP, as they will be able to teach their students how to go about writing academic texts, and especially how to deal with the conclusion sections. It also furnishes the students of Applied Linguistics, with knowledge of the genre being studied and of the set conventions of their specific area of study thus enabling them to participate successfully and effectively in the activities of their chosen disciplines.

-Moves

Swales (1990), points out that Moves are the rhetorical divisions of academic texts that convey different communicative purposes. In his Create a Research Space (CARS) model he proposes a procedure for analyzing Moves in a Research Article Introduction (henceforth RAI). He further argues that the Moves are used to reflect the writer's purpose as well as the conventions set out by the discourse community on how to write the text in question.

In his study on the article Introductions (Swales, 1981) and in the subsequent studies by analysts in the same field (Mckinlay, 1984, Dudley-Evans, 1986; Peng, 1987, Salager-Meyer, 1992, Flowerdew, 2002) Moves are seen as linguistic features that are compulsory in a text for it to be seen and accepted as belonging to a given class of genre.

In his model of the research article Introduction (RAI) Swales, (1990a:141) pays close attention to the rhetorical functions that an author aims at achieving in their text and that therefore, dictate the structure and choice of words used in the introduction. He thus, gives a framework made up of categories that are more sociological than linguistic in nature. They are as found in the figure below:

Swales' CARS model of Research Article Introduction

Move 1: Establishing a Territory
Move 2: Establishing a Niche by
Step 1A: Counter-Claiming
or
Step 1B: Indicating a Gap
or
Step 1C: Question Raising
or
Step 1D: Continuing a Tradition
Move 3: Occupying the Niche

Veronica M. Mutinda

Although this model is based on the RA introductions, a move-based approach has also been used for the analysis of other research article part genres such as the abstract (Salager-Meyer, 1990), the methods section (Wood, 1982), the results section (Brett, 1994; Williams, 1999), the discussion section (Belanger, 1982; Dudley-Evans, 1994), for analysis of dissertations (Hopkins and Dudley-Evans, 1988), and also for analysis of the structure of the thesis (Bunton, 2005; Thompson, 2001; Paltridge, 2002; Maroko, 2008). Moves in the CARS model are flexible, therefore, their results can be analyzed and discussion in RA published in journals of Applied Linguistics. A move is here taken to mean a semantic unit that helps the writer realize a given communicative purpose, (Dudley-Evans, 1986).

Nwogu further defines a "Move" as:

> "a text segment made up of a bundle of linguistic features (lexical meanings, propositional meanings, illocutionary forces and so on) which gives the segment a uniform orientation and signal the content of discourse in it," (1997:11).

For example, from the paragraph below a move *reporting results* can be identified:

> Citations from English-medium texts are clearly dominant in both EMN and EMI journals produced by Portuguese scholars, but the tendency is most marked in the EMI sub-corpus, where a total of 95.3% of citations are to texts published in English,

in contrast with 3.4% to texts published in Portuguese and 1.3% to texts in other languages.

Reporting results: *Citations* from English-medium texts *are clearly dominant in* both EMN and EMI journals produced by Portuguese scholars…

-The Results and Discussion sections

In this section a review is given of the studies related to the Results and Discussion sections which are the main concern here.

-The results section

Previous studies on this section include those by Swales (1990, 2004), Brett (1994), Williams (1994), Swales and Feak (2004), Yang and Allison (2003), Hyland (2004) and Kanoksilapathan (2007). Swales (1990), and (2004), say that the Results section involves mainly giving the background information to support the statement of results and to explain the findings using examples.

Brett (1994) studied the Results section of 20 Sociology RAs. He reports that this section points out new findings and gives the author's interpretation and comments on these findings. He describes three major Moves in terms of their linguistic features. These three Moves he calls communicative categories namely: the Metatextual, Presentation and Comment Moves. He says that the

Metatextual defines parts of the text that refer to the data or to other written sections. He says it serves to guide the reader to other parts of the work. Presentation categories, he says are those that report, present, or highlight the results and the ways in which they are obtained. He explains Comment categories as those in which authors present their interpretations of or comments and opinions about the results already presented. The Comment categories build up on the Presentation categories. He also notes that the three organizational categories occur in a cyclical manner with the metatextual (the pointer), the presentation (the statement of findings) and the comments (substantiating the findings) pattern being the most commonly noted pattern. The three Moves are also reported by Posteguillo (1999) in his investigation into the Results sections of Computer Science RAs. Posteguillo also reports in his study that the Moves found in RAs in Computer Science are frequently recycled.

From the reviewed studies it is clear that the Results sections of the RAs of the two disciplines report and comment on results and that these two moves of reporting and commenting on results occur in a cyclical pattern.

Williams (1999) using Brett's model of communicative categories as a yardstick examined a sample of 8 medical RAs. He found Brett's model adequate for the rhetorical structure of Results sections, but reported that moves in biochemistry articles did not appear in a cyclical presentation as reported by Brett. He reported that the Presentation of the Results sections of biomedical articles tended to be more linear. Williams thus suggests that the structural organization of an article is dictated upon by the type of study as well as the subject matter being studied.

Yang and Allison (2003) in an approach to studying the organizational patterns of Results and Discussion sections studied 20 Applied Linguistics articles. They reported a six -move pattern for the Results section: preparatory information, reporting results, summarizing results, commenting on results, evaluating the study and deduction from the research. They say that the first three are the most dominant moves.

Kanoksilapatham (2007) examined the Results section of 60 biochemistry articles. She reported four moves (that may vary in order and occur cyclically) for organizing content: restating methodological issues, justifying methodological issues, announcing results, and commenting on results. She notes that each of the moves contains sub-moves called steps. For each step a sentence is given to describe the function of the step in its content-organizing role.

Many earlier studies have studied the structural organization of texts by looking into their linguistic categories of organization or by specifically analyzing the moves used to constitute the rhetorical structure of a text. These researchers then related these rhetorical structures to the linguistic features that make these texts up. In the different patterns proposed by the different researchers, there are some similarities as well as differences between structures found in different disciplines but reporting and commenting on results are seen to be the most integral moves in the majority of disciplines studied (Bruce 2008).

In this book, I deal in depth on the Results sections of RAs in Applied Linguistics with the aim of providing communicative categories and their organization into rhetorical structures as well as linking the communicative categories to their particular linguistic features. I also look into the rhetorical structure of the Results sections of RAs in Applied Linguistics journals corresponding to those reported by Brett and other studies reviewed. I conclude that a Results section reports results and comments on results, and that these two moves appear in a cyclic pattern.

-The Discussion Section

Swales and Feak (1994) in an academic writing textbook observed that the position of the Discussion section in the text implies that the audience have read and understood all the earlier parts of the text. Rasmeenin (2006) reports that some RA authors may introduce this section by answering questions and others will choose to begin the section by giving a summary of the findings or by stating the principal findings. He observes that this is a clear indicator that there is no conventionally agreed-upon pattern for structuring this section thus the reason as to why the section lacks a uniform structure. This means that the section needs to be studied further.

Yang and Desmond (2002) reported that the Discussion section is structured in the same exact pattern as the Introduction section in terms of structure in that it should move from the specific to a general view of how the results in the Methods and Results sections should be interpreted. Swales (2004) gives the three-move CARS structure for the Introduction section and says the Discussion is also presented in the same structure. Yang and Desmond (2002) and Holmes (1997) have indicated that this section presents its moves from the specific to the general in a cyclical manner.

I endeavored to analyze and reveal the communicative purposes of the Discussion section of RAs published in journals of Applied Linguistics. I also sought to establish if this section is a mirror image of the Introduction as Swales (1990) and Yang and Desmond (2002) say, that is to find out if it follows the CARS model of the RA Introductions.

-Theoretical Framework

One of the concerns of text analysis is to provide an analysis of structure of written and spoken texts. This necessitates a need to investigate the rhetorical structure of the results and conclusion sections of RAs in journals of Applied Linguistics.

-Genre Theory

Genre Theory and genre studies began with the Greeks in the 18th Century who observed that the kind of work that a writer produced solely depended on the writer's personality. They also believed that certain linguistic forms were meant for certain genres and not suitable for use in others. This theory began as a classification system in the 18th C Greece.

The theory underwent many changes and since the 18th Century linguists have been working towards getting a theory of genre that would be more suited to studying the different forms and structures of individual texts within genres. Genre underwent a lot of evolution through the 19th and 20th Centuries.

Coe et al. (2002) state that this theory arose from attempts by researchers to understand writing as a social activity. They also point out that it arose in an effort to analyze texts and understand the nature of academic discourse. One of this theory's key focus is to describe the major organizational characteristics of different kinds of writing (or speaking), that are key for the author(s) to fully participate in the academic world and to function efficiently in the wider society.

Macken et al. (1990) say that the label 'genre' is, is not all that important in itself, except by the fact it serves to establish a relationship between the genre analysis study approach and rhetoric – an approach of linguistics study dating back to the days of Aristotle. They report that of importance is the many ideas that genre holds concerning writing, speaking and language, which are key to understanding genre-theory and their impact on literacy and education in general.

The first idea is that genres are social activities that serve certain communicative purposes and that these communicative purposes guide the writing of genres. The first notable and most important observation is that to use language either spoken or written is a social function which thus makes language a social phenomenon. This makes writing and speaking to be considered as social activities. From the above observation we can then conclude that everything about language usage has a social reason that is meant to realize a certain effect in the audience – readers and/or listeners. Language usage has to do with our choice of words and phrases, sentence types and paralinguistic features to the types of texts which are dictated upon by the social environment in which we write. This is because certain types of texts are a domain of given discourse situations.

Secondly, this theory holds that speaking and writing are social practices. This is to say that they have to be undertaken and studied in relation to other social activities in and around which they occur. Speaking and writing cannot occur and/or be studied in isolation while ignoring other social practices surrounding them. Of key importance to note is the fact that, genres identify very closely with social factors such as class, gender, age, ethnicity, and geographic location.

The third idea under this theory is that language occurs as text and text has a rhetorical structure. According to Swales (2004), genre is seen as communicative events, defined by well-defined set of communicative purposes that are known and understood by the members of the discourse community in question and in which they regularly appear. Whenever we use language to either speak or write, we operate in given social situations. This means that our choice of what language structures to use depends on the situation we are operating in and so dictates what we say and how we say it.

The use of language is governed by routine and conventions which dictate what is said/written and when. Therefore, speaking and writing calls for ones understanding of the governing rules which state how to operate effectively and efficiently in a given genre. This is to say that language use, both spoken and written occurs in the form of a complete text, as a meaningful event which has its completeness in interacting with other social aspects in the discourse situation in which the genre occurs.

Genre is also seen as a coherent text that carries a social meaning. This means that a particular genre uses a language that is dictated upon by the situation in which it occurs thus, making language to always occur as a text that draws its meaning from its social context. Given the stability of social structures, social contexts recur, and the reasons and focus of participants in these social situations are somewhat regular to a level where they are predictable (for example having studied several RAs, a researcher is likely to find it a bit easy to study more RAs in future and to predict their rhetorical structures). This is because the texts in this genre have a certain stability and predictability when it comes to writing/producing them.

Summary

This chapter discussed the history of text analyses and the different approaches used in studying the text. It also served to provide an explanation of the basic terms and concepts (for example genre and genre analysis, and moves) as used here. Lastly the chapter explained the theoretical framework that guided me in analyzing its data.

CHAPTER THREE

Research Design and Methodology In Applied Liguistics

Introduction

In this chapter I explain some research methods which are employed to analyze the subject of study in applied linguistics. I endeavor to explain the research design used in analyzing the rhetorical structure of the results and discussion sections of the RAs. I also give a description of the subject, sampling procedures, data collection instruments and procedures are pointed out.

The Research Design

One research design to guide such study is the situated qualitative design- a design whose purpose and focus is to understand the meaning people have constructed (Merriam, 2009) in their written and spoken presentations. These include field notes, letters, interviews, conversations, debates, recordings, memos, journal and newspaper articles and so on, (Denzin & Lincoln, 2003). This design is best suited to investigating RAs reporting on empirical research (from direct observation of phenomena). The design is deductive and, therefore, enables the researchers tackle the study's assumptions.

The situated qualitative design is is the kind of research design that collects, interprets and presents data objectively while treating all the research subjects (RAs' Results and Conclusion sections) as homogeneous, (Atkinson, 2005). Denzin & Lincoln (2003) say that qualitative researchers study the phenomena in its natural setting and attempt to interpret and understand phenomena in regard to the meaning(s) that people put to them.

Cohen (2007) reports that this research design employs several methods in collecting data and that this design also makes the data real and easy to understand in depth and thus helps make sense of the phenomena that the researcher is studying. McMillan, et al (2001) and Connole, et al (1993) note that this design is central to most approach that are interpretive in nature. Waltham (1993) says that an interpretive design is a method of research that starts from the position where our knowledge is. Employing this kind of research design, the researcher sets off with the knowledge gained from earlier studies in applied linguistics and goes ahead to study the results and conclusion sections of RAs to establish their rhetorical structure which is dictated upon by the discourse community in which the author is operating.

The qualitative researcher analyses words rather than rely on statistical procedures and they also analyze the words to place them into larger meanings for easy interpretation and comprehension. These larger grouping include categories and themes, (Creswell, 2012). By so doing, one can investigate the RA in journals of applied linguistics to analyze words into categories labeled 'moves' that form a rhetorical structure of results and conclusion sections of the RA.

This design is advantageous because one of its strengths is that it allows for greater (theoretically informed) flexibility, (Silverman, 2005) and that it also enables the researcher to conduct a thorough study and thus better-informed, studies on a greater range of topics in easy to understand and everyday terms, (Yin, 2011).

This design also allows the researcher to work with a relatively small number of cases:

> "Qualitative researchers typically study a relatively small number of individuals or situations and preserve the individuality of each of these in their analyses rather than collecting data from large samples and aggregating the data across individuals or situations."

> (Maxwell, 1996, p.17)

Storus (2015), reports that the qualitative method is a systematic, subjective approach used to describe life experiences such as academic writing and give them meaning. One can investigate the results and conclusion sections of RAs in applied linguistics journals and try to make meaning of the rhetorical structure employed by the authors.

Yin (2011) says that the qualitative research method comprises of five major types of designs: phenomenology, ethnography, case study research, the grounded theory and historical research designs. The case study design studies phenomena in its real-world context while the grounded theory aims to generate and develop a theory from collected data to explain how and why a phenomenon is as is.

Storus (2015) says that qualitative research employs four major methods of collecting data: participating in the setting, observing phenomena directly, in-depth interviewing and analyzing documents and materials. One can use the last method of data analyses mentioned here to analyze documents (RAs sections). This makes research design discussed very informative and helpful due to the attributes of the method discussed here.

Sampling Procedures and Sample Size

One of the sources of research data in is to draw from RAs published in journals in Applied Linguistics. According to *The Linguist List of Journals* (2012), there are thirty categories of journals in linguistics and related areas. Of these thirty categories the researcher would focus on Applied Linguistics. This discipline is of particular interest for pedagogic reasons, because part of its disciplinary content is raising awareness of genre features.

Out of thousands of journals published in Applied Linguistics, the corpus can be built from ten (10) established journals of in this field. These are purposively sampled from the list of journals in Applied Linguistics that the researcher' institution subscribes to. Applied linguistics is an area that is very diverse and, therefore, of main focus can be limited to the sub-field that deals with English language teaching. Then issues printed in a particular year are selected especially the most recent then and therefore, likely to carry any recent developments in the rhetorical move structure of the RA genre. This will enable the researchers to avoid generational and diachronic changes that are possible in such a dynamic genre as the RA. From the identified issues a RA (an article that is of relevance to the readership of English language education) can purposively be chosen. These articles are then randomly numbered: RA1, RA2 ... RA10.

For example:

a.) *International Journal of Applied Linguistics (IJAL),*
b.) *Modern Journal of Applied Linguistics (MJAL),*
c.) *Applied Linguistics Review (ALR),*
d.) *Second Language Research (SLR),*
e.) *Journal of Applied Language Studies (Apples),*
f.) *Studies in Second Language Acquisition (SSLA), and Language Learning Journal (LLJ),*
g.) *Journal of ELT and Applied Linguistics (JELTAL),*
h.) *Journal of Applied Linguistics and Professional Practice (JALPP),*
i.) *International Journal of Applied Linguistics and English Literature (IJALEL),*
j.) *Annual Review of Applied Linguistics (ARAL)*

Data collection procedures

Data from the Results and Conclusions sections of the RAs identified are collected by extracting the complete Results and Conclusions sections. This provides raw data on the results and discussion sections which are then used to investigate the Moves adopted by the writer in each section. To identify the rhetorical moves, the sentences in each section are analyzed to find out what the author aims to communicate or do with language. For instance, the researchers aim could be to find out and record what communicative purpose (what the author aims to communicate) the RA author had aimed to achieve in his choice of language. What the author intends to communicate to the readers determines what words will be used and how the language used is structured which then shapes the communicative purpose of the said author.

Using the communicative purpose as a basis, each move is studied to identify the verbs that signal the purposes and then the rhetorical structure of the sections is identified. The Moves established are then analyzed to determine the general functions of the sections, for example: reporting, commenting, and comparing (results). Then a comparing and contrasting exercise is carried out on the rhetorical structures identified to find out the similarities and differences in terms of the communicative purposes/ functions of the sections.

Data analysis

Units of analysis are identified on the basis of communicative purposes with reference to the conventional functional headings (e.g. Results), and other varied functional headings taken to correspond to the conventional headings (e.g. Findings). The communicative purposes thus enable the researcher to identify the Moves used in these sections.

An analysis of the texts in the corpus is carried out to get the Moves. First the individual sentences of each text excerpt can be rewritten in a scrapbook in order to separate the sentences of the text before any analysis begins (Njoroge, 1996). Nwogu (1997) gives guide on process of identification of Moves. This involves:

a.) Focusing on the propositions in the texts and identifying important information.

b.) Searching for linguistic clues such as function words, explicit lexemes and expressions, verb forms, discourse conjuncts and markers, structural headings and subheadings, summary statements etc.

c.) Classifying and paraphrasing the context of discourse based on the linguistic clues.

d.) Assigning discourse functions to the overall information in segments of text as well as constituent elements of information in the segments.

e.) Establishing whether or not the function identified is general by reference to other texts in the corpus.

After identifying the Moves occurring in each RA results and discussion section the frequencies of occurrence and the percentage of all types of Moves in each of the sections are calculated. The rhetorical structure of the sections under study is outlined by investigating what the RA authors were trying to do in the relevant sections. The relevant unit of analysis is the Move (Swales, 1990, 2004). This is done by looking at the ideational relations that hold between the sections based on the implied meaning or explicit linguistic signals present. The rhetorical relations in the various groups identified are described in functional terms depending on the communicative role of each group. This is followed by a deductive description of the general functions of the sections as per the Moves identified and the similarities and differences between the communicative purposes of the sections are elicited.

Av researcher can adopt explicit and self-explanatory language to identify and label the Moves. To do this, the V+ing phrases are used if the study is focused on identifying what the RA authors were trying to do with the discourse. For example, reporting results, or comparing results with literature review.

Summary

This section has provided an elaboration on the research design and the sampling procedures which can be used by a researcher in applied linguistics. It has also explained how the researcher can identify the journals in the field of Applied Linguistics and specifically the area that deals with English Language education and how to purposively select the specific research articles to be used to provide the corpus. It has also explained how the results and discussions sections can be cut from the original RA and then the sentences analyzed to enable the researcher to identify the rhetorical structure of the sections under study.

CHAPTER FOUR

Results and Discussion

Introduction

This chapter deals with the issue of the findings. First a description is provided of the rhetorical structure of the Results and Discussion sections as dictated by the communicative functions discovered in each section, then the rhetorical functions served by the Results and Discussion sections are described and finally an examination of the rhetorical structures of the two sections for any similarities and differences is provided.

Rhetorical Move Structure of the Results Section

Here, a Move is used to refer to a semantic unit that mirrors the writer's purpose (Dudley-Evans, 1986; Wirada & Wannaruk, 2013) and signals the content of discourse in it (Nwogu, 1997). A move is also seen as a rhetorical division of academic texts that conveys the writer's communicative purposes and reflects the conventions of the discourse community, (Swales, 1990).

Six rhetorical moves are identified in the corpus of Results sections as shown in Table 4.2 below. The findings on the rhetorical structure of the results section agree with Yang and Allison's (2003) 6-Moves RA Results Moves (henceforth Results Move- RM):

Results Sections

Table 4.1 (below) presents the current findings on Moves in terms of the number of times each Move occurred in the results sections of our corpus as well as the average frequency each move occurred in the results section.

Table: Moves in Applied Linguistics RA Results Sections

Moves	Frequency(n)	Percentage
RM1 – Preparatory Information	41	4.1
RM2 – Reporting Results	566	56.8
RM3- Commenting on Results	238	23.9
RM4 – Summarizing Results	132	13.3
RM5 – Evaluating the study	12	1.2
RM6 – Deductions from the study	7	0.7

Total	**N**= 996	100

NB: To determine the percentage we used the formula n/N × 100

Where each item e.g. RM1 = n

The aggregate frequency = N

Percentage = n/N × 100

As mentioned earlier, this concurs with Yang & Allison's (2003) move structure framework on the moves found in the results section although with a difference on which Move is the most dominant and obligatory. Of the six Moves, Moves 2 (Reporting Results), Move 3 (Commenting on Results) and Move 4 (Summarizing Results) are found to occur at a higher frequency in all the RAs than the rest of the moves identified. This is unlike Yang and Allison's study which found Moves 1(Preparatory Information), Move 2 (Reporting Results) and Move 3 (Commenting on Results) to be the most dominant moves with Move 2 (Reporting Results) and Move 3 (Commenting on Results) being obligatory in the results section of a RA in Applied Linguistics.

It should be pointed out that the authors could report and discuss results without necessarily pointing out to all instances of reporting results thus RM4 (Summarizing Results) appeared at a higher frequency than RM1 (Preparatory Information).

From the done analysis the following can be asserted:

RM1 - Preparatory information

The researcher would agree with Yang & Allison (2003) in noting that this move restates the methods and instruments the researchers used to get the results. The researcher would also concur that this move also directs the reader to tables and/or graphs that display results in the RA.

This move is found to mainly point out where results are to be found in the results section and to also compare results with literature review. It serves as a pointer and reminder to the reader that results are being presented. It is an introductory stage that precedes the presentation of results as signaled by such examples as the following:

Descriptive statistics are applied to answer the first research question... (RA2)

The number of *examples of* self-discrepancy found for each is presented in *Figure 1*... (RA5)

The data are analyzed using *mixed models of covariance...* (RA8)

Prior to the interview, the interpreter initiates *a dialogue, (extract1)*, about the procedure. (RA6)

The authors as seen in the text extract prepare the reader to receive the results by pointing to where in the results section the results are to be found i.e. it points to extract(s), example(s), graph(s) and discussion(s) that present the findings of the study. For instance, in example 2, the author talks of a *figure1* that presents the results of the studied phenomena and example 1 restates that the author used *'descriptive statistics'* as a method used to answer the research questions just as Yang and Allison's (2003) say RM1 should.

RM2 – Reporting results

This move is founded on presentation of findings and support the findings with data in form of tables, graphs and examples and also by description (Yang and Allison, 2003). It presents the outcome in the study as exemplified below:

> *The response times analysis was* initially based on… (RA8)

> *Nigerian dress is* "an idiosyncratic symbol" which… (RA9)

> *For the self-discrepancy code, 172 quotations were found.* (RA5)

> *'Reversals' are identified,* specific turn patterns aimed at consensus. (RA3)

From the examples above the authors are seen to present the results of their research. The results are presented in one or a combination of the forms mentioned earlier: graphs, description, figures, tables, and examples. As seen in example 7; the author presents the findings of the study in terms of numbers: *172 quotations…* and example 6 gives a *description* of the Nigerian dress.

RM3 - Commenting on results

Yang & Allison (2003) say that this move establishes the meaning and significance of the findings presented in Move 2 (reporting results) in relation to the related field of study. This move's function could for instance be used to interpret Move 2 (reporting results) by giving explanations and illustrations. It can also be asserted that move 3 serves to mention the significance of the findings presented in Move 2 (Reporting Results) in relation to the objectives of the researcher. That is to say that RM3 relates the findings to the hypothesis/assumptions – what the researcher had set out to find and what are the findings of the current study (Yang and Allison, 2003). This move tells the reader if the findings were expected or unexpected.

It also serves to elaborate the results by explaining what (new) idea they contribute to the field of study and to what extent are the results generalizable to the discipline studied. Here the researcher also compares results with literature review by reviewing earlier research work in the same field and saying which earlier research agrees with the current findings. Some examples on this move drawn from the study's data would include:

This finding is similar to the study conducted by... (RA2)

This is in congruence with the findings of the study done by... (RA2)

Suggests there is a discrepancy between the available latitude for categorization and decision making. (RA3)

Both of the control groups behaved as expected (on the basis of claims from the literature). (RA4)

In examples 9 and 10 the authors compare their work with earlier research work by use of such words as '*is similar to...*' and '*is in congruence with..*' and example 11 suggests a new idea/finding by the current study: '*a discrepancy...*' This move will also mention if the results agree with the assumptions of the study: '*as expected...*'(example 12).

RM4 - Summarizing results

Just like Yang and Allison (2003) such study explained here would be found to have established that this move is usually a summarized form of Move 2(Reporting Results) and Move 3(Commenting on Results). As such, it can be asserted that It briefly restates the finding and generalizes the results in what we could also call 'topic generalization.' (The author states how useful the findings of the on-going study are to the area of study). These functions are supported by the examples below:

I think that I need to *have a value of universalism and conformity to support intercultural communication*. (RA5)

Because the *effects were only visible in the accuracy scores and not in the response times*, it could have been the case that speed was sacrificed for accuracy. (RA 8)

Dress culture, therefore, *promotes a culture of seniority based on achievement and desire for success*. (RA9)

In the examples above, the authors briefly state the findings of the study and their significance to the field of study. Example on dress culture, for instance summarizes the study's findings on dress culture by using the signal word: *therefore,* followed briefly by mentioning the importance of the findings.

The remaining moves - RM5 (evaluating the study) and RM6 (deduction from the study), serve to conclude the Results section.

RM5: Evaluating the study

This is a move that Yang and Allison (2003) found to briefly mention the principal results and their interpretation and/ or meaning. The author would also concur that this move evaluates the success of the study in terms of limitations in application of the results as in the examples below:

> It should be noted, however, that *this effect is mainly restricted to the data from third grade,* as there was no difference between the L1 and L2 learners in sixth grade with respect to their accuracy on regular and irregular verbs compared to L1 learners. (RA8)

> Only with *such more studies will we be able to determine how generalizable its claims truly are. (RA10)*

> It can be understood that *advanced learners have a strong tendency towards using determination techniques* because of their adequate knowledge of English and better English comprehension. (RA2)

This is an *obvious limitation* for testing its claims as being more general... (RA10)

From the examples above, the researcher would report that this move serves to conclude the study by mentioning and interpreting the results briefly and by indicating the success and limitations of the current study's findings. For instance, Example 16 in the texts states the limitation of the study's results saying the results are *'restricted'* to a certain level of learning and example 17 mentions the need for *'more studies'* in order to be able to generalize the findings of the on-going study. Example 18 serves to briefly mention the results, *'learners have a tendency to...'* and interprets the results, *'because...'* All these examples agree with literature reviewed namely: Yang & Allison's (2003) move structure model on Results sections which served as the study's standard model in the analysis of the Results section.

RM6 – Deductions from the study

This is the move that identifies gaps (for further study) related to but not addressed by the current study (Yang and Allison, 2003). This move also gives the study's implications as seen in the following examples drawn from the corpus:

This observation suggests that cognitive notions of grammar may also *need to be re-specified...* (RA8)

Proponents of CEM would do well in *future research to address these and related concerns* for this model. (RA10)

> Providing the *chance to engage in lucrative professional learning opportunities* increases the likelihood that teachers will *reflect on their practice, identify contradictions, generate solutions with colleagues and experiment with alternative approaches.* (RA1)

With this move, the author points to the need for other researchers to areas related to the present study that need to be studied either because they have not been studied or are not extensively researched. This is as seen in for instance: Example 21 requesting for '*future research*' to look at concerns raised and example 20 seeking to have future researchers '*re-specify*' a certain finding of the on-going study. The authors also tell the reader what changes need to be effected in the field of study as per the new idea(s) suggested by the findings of the current study as example 22 of the presented data talk about '*experiment with…*' This suggests that there is a new idea presented by the current study.

So far, the study should be seen to agree with previous studies (Yang & Allison, 2003) on the moves and communicative purposes served by the results section of a RA; however, the findings of the study noted that it found Move 2, (Reporting Results), Move 3 (Commenting on Results) and Move 4 (Summarizing Results) to be obligatory in RAs results sections unlike Yang & Allison's (2003) study that found Move 2 (Reporting Results) and Move 3 (Commenting on Results) to be the only moves that were obligatory. The moves are labelled as obligatory if they are found to have a higher frequency than the rest in the rhetorical structure and if they are found in all the RA sections studied.

The presented study should be opined to find the above-mentioned three moves to occur at a very high frequency in comparison to the rest of moves found in this section. Move 2 (Reporting results) had an average frequency of 56.6 and was found in all results sections. It had the highest frequency of all the six Moves. Move 3(Commenting on Results) had the next highest frequency with a mean of 23.8 and Move 4 (Summarizing Results) took position three with a mean frequency of 13.2 and the fourth in frequency was Move 5 (Evaluating the Study) with a mean of 4.1.

It is also found that reporting results and commenting on results (Move 2 and Move 3 respectively) were the dominant moves in the Results section and that the focus of this section presents the findings of an on-going study.

Move 2 (Reporting Results), Move 3 (Commenting on Results), and Move 4 (Summarizing Results) occurred in all the Results sections and at a higher frequency than the others in the section under study. This means they are obligatory for a Results section of a RA to be said to be complete. Though Move 5 (Evaluating the Study) occurred at a noticeably low frequency it was noted that Applied Linguists felt obliged to evaluate their study and so they took time to move outside their work and outline the significance of their work.

Move 1 (Preparatory Information) although occurring at a lower frequency (a mean of 1.2) was found in seven out of the ten RAs. Most Results sections had at least one instance of preparatory information and others more than one instance of occurrence but this does not make the Move obligatory since it does not occur in all RAs. For instance, the results section of RA9 delves directly into the business of reporting results (Move 2) without any preamble as seen in the extracts presented below from the data as:

1.   Semiotics and Dress culture, a branch of linguistic anthropology, according to…. (RA9)

The example above is the opening statement of the Results section in RA9 and throughout the RA the author directly presents the results without pointing them out. It is felt this was because of the nature of the study as it was more descriptive than statistical. The author is explaining a certain phenomenon-why it is as is.

There were RAs without a Move 6 (Deduction from the results). This move is also not obligatory since it was found in only four RAs (RA3, RA7, RA8 and RA10) with a frequency mean of 0.7 meaning that not all Results sections recommended areas for further study.

As can be seen in Table 4.2 the Results sections mainly focuses on presenting the findings of the study and explaining the findings in relation to earlier studies (comparing results with literature review) as well as accounting for the results (by explaining how/methodology for obtaining the results) (Swales, 1990; Yang & Allison, 2003; Kanoksilatham, 2005). This is due to the high frequency of occurrence of Moves 2 (Reporting results), Move 3 (Commenting on results) and Move 4 (Summarizing results)

The order of the Moves in the Results sections is as presented in Table 4.2 – moving from Move 1 to Move

6. In the RA where Move 1 is missing Move 2 begins the rhetorical structure and the other Moves follow.

This section is notably very cyclical in terms of Moves as the author presents the findings of the study. There are some cyclic patterns concerning moves in the results sections. The typical pattern is: M1M2M3M4M5M6 although this pattern is not linear and straightforward. Moves 2 and 3 were highly cyclical with the two occurring many times before the author decided to summarize the findings (RM4) and then evaluate the study (RM5) and make deductions from the study (RM6).

In conclusion it is observed that the RA Results section in the corpus agrees with previous studies on the same sections by Williams (1999), and Nwogu (1997) in medicine, Kanoksilapatham (2005) in biochemistry, Posteguillo (1999) in computer science and Brett (1994) in Sociology and Yang an Allison (2003) in Applied Linguistics. All these studies found that RA Results sections focus on two major issues: Reporting and commenting on findings. But the main communicative focus of this section is to report results.

Therefore, it is true to say that RA Results section in applied linguistics report results and comment on results and the author adds here the idea that, after commenting on results, the authors will also summarize the results. The author also concludes that all the RAs had Move 5 (Evaluating the study) though at a lower frequency than Moves 2, 3, and 4. All the researchers indicated the importance of their study- the study's contribution to the academic pool in the field of study.

Rhetorical Move Structure of the Discussion Section

The author set out to illustrate an investigation of the rhetorical structure of the RA Discussion section with Swales' (1990) CARS Model as the main point of reference and goes on to show that this model does not cater for most of the moves identified in the corpus. Therefore, after extensive research in the field of genre analysis of the RA, the author points out more recent and extensive studies on the rhetorical structure of the RA sections and especially the Discussion section (Swales and Feak, 1994; Holmes, 1997; Peacock, 2002; Yang and Allison, 2002, 2003; Swales, 2004; and Rasmeenin, 2006; Peng, 1987; Hopkins & Dudley-Evans, 1988; Kanoksilapatham, 2005). The author goes further to establish the rhetorical structure of the discussion section and compare with earlier move models proposed to see which one this her analysis agrees with. She finally settled on the Yang and Allison (2003) Move-Structure framework, though not the only framework available (see above), coincidentally, most studies in this field of study agree it is the most comprehensive.

The Yang and Allison (2003) Move model is the most preferred because it belongs to Applied Linguistics since it is worth noting that disciplinary variations in terms of communicative purposes and use of language do exist (Holmes, 1997; Nwogu, 1997; Kanokslapatham, 2005). In addition, this move model is an extension and modification of several other earlier models which makes it quite informative.

Therefore, with a significant number of other researchers in the field of applied linguistics, the author is reliably aligned to Yang and Allison's (2003) move analysis framework on discussions than the rest of the models available.

Yang and Allison (2003) framework proposes seven rhetorical moves in the discussion section as follows:

DM1 – Background information
DM2 – Reporting results
DM3 – Summarizing results
DM4 – Commenting on results
DM5 – Summarizing the study
DM6 – Evaluating the study
DM7 – Deduction from the research

Unlike Yang and Allison's (2003) model which proposes seven moves, the author further found the discussion section to have six rhetorical moves: Background information, Summarizing results, Commenting on results, Summarizing the study, Evaluating the study and Deductions from the research. She differs with the model by Yang and Allison (2003) on discussion Move 2 (Reporting results) and Move 3 (Summarizing results).

According to the author, Move 2 deals with summarizing results unlike Yang and Allison's, (2003) model that identified reporting results and summarizing reports as two distinct moves in the Discussion section. She finds the discussion section to be summarizing the results that have already been reported in the results section. This section presents a summarized form of the results discussed earlier in the results section without discussing particular results and the factors that led to their realization.

Just like with the Results section, the sentence was the unit of analysis in the study of the discussion sections. This study deciphered what communicative purpose(s) the author had assigned each sentence and in the few cases where the sentence had more than one move, it split the sentence to indicate the author's intention. The analysis of this author reports realizing six moves in the discussion sections of the corpus which were labeled as Discussion Move1-6 (henceforth DM1-6). The findings of such study on the discussion sections are presented in table below.

Table: Moves in Applied Linguistics RA Discussion sections

Moves	Frequency(n)	Percentage
DM 1- Background information	14	3.5
DM2 – Summarizing results	53	13.1
DM3 – Commenting on results	263	64.8
DM4 – Summarizing the study	31	7.6
DM5 – Evaluating the study	29	7.1
DM6 – Deductions from the study	16	3.9
TOTAL	**N** = 406	100

NB: To determine the percentage one uses the formula n/N × 100

Where each item e.g. RM1 = n

The aggregate frequency = N

Percentage = n/N × 100

As shown in Table above, Move 3 (Commenting on results) is the most frequent move in the corpus followed by Move 2 (Summarizing results). These two moves (Move 2 and Move 3) are found to be obligatory. Move 1(Background Information) and Move 6(Deductions from the study) are found to be optional in the discussion section as per the frequency of occurrence – 14% and 16% respectively. The author focuses on summarizing the results and commenting on results, summarizing the study and finally on evaluating the study. These would be the integral parts of a discussion section of a RA in Applied Linguistics.

The rhetorical moves identified by such study and their realizations are discussed below:

DM 1: Background Information

This move prepares the reader for the discussion of results to come and also gives statements such as a summary of the research questions and objectives of the study as well as gives the theoretical background and research methodology (Weissberg & Buker, 1990; Yang & Allison, 2003). The author would concur with Nodoushan (2012), who reports that authors use metadiscursive elements or metatext to signal this move to the readers (such as 'the aim of this was to...). This move would be found to be optional with a very low frequency of occurrence. The writer will find it appropriate to use present and past simple tenses to present this move. This move can be shown in the examples that follow:

2. The present *study addresses the* ... (RA7)

25. In the present study *the target words are* ... (RA7)

26. In the following I *will discuss* ... (RA3)

27. The formal linguistic models of L3 transfer reviewed *in this article exemplify...* (RA10)

28. Our topic, namely, *how the process of small group based planning work focusing on grammatical accuracy in IFL is achieved* in the moment and over time, is *of independent interest to* both cognitive SLA and CA. (RA8)

As shown in the examples above, this move helps the author to let the reader know in a summarized form what the study is all about. It will be found that a reader can easily know what the study is about by reading the discussion section of a RA without necessarily having to read the whole research work.

This move makes that possible as it restates the research questions, objectives, and the theoretical background as well as mentions the research methodology (see examples 26,

27 and 28). Examples 24, 25 and 26 restate the objective of the study: *'study addresses...', 'target words are...'* and *'will discuss...'* and example 27 mentions the research methodology used in the study: *'linguistic model of...'*

DM 2: Summarizing Results

This move is indicated by use of reporting and summarizing verbs, statements with numerical values and pointing to graphs, tables and examples as well as observations and comments on the expectedness and unexpectedness of the results (Rasmeenin, 2006). The authors use this move to present a summed-up version of the results mentioned earlier in the results section. It presents results and is frequently followed by Move 3 (commenting on results). Just like Move 1(Preparatory Information), this move is presented in both the present and past simple tenses and the passive voice. This can be argued to be the second most frequent move in the analysis of the discussion section and as exemplified in examples 29-32 below:

29. A number of sociolinguistic *factors which determine one's dress have been highlighted and discussed. They include*: time of the day, season, social events, religious tradition, economic and political consideration... (RA9)

30. *In summarizing* generative research with a particular emphasis on transfer at the L3/Ln initial stages... (RA10)

31. *We have shown* (contrary to the traditional understanding of planning in cognitive SLA) *that planning is an observable process at least in social terms.* (RA 8)

32. *The behavior of* the Spanish group *was generally in line with expectations based on claims in the literature.* (RA4)

This move serves to sum up the findings of an on-going study as supported by example 30 which uses the summing up word: *'summarizing'.* The move also mentions the core business of the specific study: For example; to research a hypothesis by either confirming earlier findings by other studies according to the literature reviewed or come up with new idea(s). For instance, here extract text number 31 presents a new idea indicated by use of the contrasting phrase, *'contrary to'* and example 32 compares the findings of the study with previous literature reviewed and indicates that the findings were *'in line with expectations based on claims in literature.'*

DM 3: Commenting on results

This move interprets results through comparing them with previous studies (Rasmeenin, 2006) and gives reasons for observed differences (if any). The function of this move is that of elaborating the results by bringing out their meaning and significance in relation to the field of study. This move also evaluates results by stating their strengths and weaknesses and then it proceeds to make generalizations of the results to the field of study. The reporter or researcher uses the first -person pronoun 'we' and the present simple tense in the passive form to realize this move as seen in the following examples:

33. *We therefore argue that* the conversation analyses of word and grammar presented here *may provide empirical insight into how* massively occurring, naturalistic, socially distributed language learning behavior ... (RA8)

34. *As we see it, the models can be taken to stem from these basic tenets, yet their respective interpretations on how these underlying driving factors play out differ,* resulting in their partially overlapping, yet crucially distinctive predictions. (RA10)

35. Transforming practice is not straightforward and may be particularly challenging for career teachers who have been teaching and learning within one context for years and now find themselves in a starkly different context. (RA1)

DM3 grounds the study by stating the significance of the findings to the field of study as seen in example 33. This is done by comparing current results with previous studies in the area of study and by explaining any new findings. Example 33 of the sample texts presents a new idea and its significance of *'providing empirical insight...'* This move also states any challenges faced with application of the findings and the strengths and weaknesses of the study's findings i.e. it says to what extent the findings of the study are generalizable as seen in example 35 which talks about a practice been *'particularly challenging'.*

This move has the highest frequency of occurrence here and so is considered obligatory. The researcher agrees with previous studies (Wirrada and Wannaruk, 2013; Nodoushan, 2012), Yang and Allison, 2003) that this move is obligatory and cyclical. It would therefore be concluded that this move has such a high frequency as compared to the other moves in the Discussion section because it is the integral function of the section to discuss, comment and explain the findings of the specific study.

DM 4: Summarizing the study

This move is unlike move 2 that summarizes the results of the study. It is an optional move that uses summary or conclusive phrases followed by a statement of results and are very often found at the end of discussions (Yang and Allison, 2003). Rasmeenin, (2006) notes that authors use lexico-grammatical signals such as the present perfect tense together with words such as 'study/research.' The researcher's analysis would find this move to be providing the reader with statements that sum up the whole study. The following are examples that are drawn from the data:

> 36. *From this standpoint,* the uncritical promotion of the Ideal L2 Self by nurturing such desires solely to increase L2 motivation… (RA5)

> 37. *Finally,* as L2 learners acquire more experience with the auditory input and increase attention to the

phonological forms in the input, they could abstract important phonological rules from the input and construct phonological representations in the mental lexicon and use them to identify words in various contexts. (RA7)

38. *Finally*, teacher-directed approaches to professional development enable teachers to "move beyond being not only consumers of top- down expert knowledge, but also producers of school-based, self- directed knowledge by adopting a 'researcher' lens." (RA1)

As can be seen from the examples above, this move sums up the whole study by using words such as '*from this standpoint,*' (example 36) and '*finally*' in examples 37 and 38. It helps the authors tie together the research by summarizing the findings and relating them to the objectives of the on-going study (see example 36 where the study's objective is to *increase L2 motivation* and example 37 aimed at enabling learners to *acquire experience ….. to identify words*).

DM 5: Evaluating the study

The objective of this move is to point out the strengths and weaknesses of the methodology used in the study (Yang and Allison, 2003; Nodoushan, 2012). This move also evaluates the study by mentioning the contributions of the study to the academic pool in the field of study and by highlighting the limitations of the present study and its findings. To do this the author uses both the present and past simple tenses. This move is optional since its frequency of occurrence was quite low; (7%). See the examples (drawn from study's data) below:

39. *The data supporting this is gathered in a business context* where human lives or comfort are not at stake, but perhaps it is not inconceivable that there are situations also in a healthcare context where the development of options in the decision-making process might benefit from using similar discourse strategies. (RA3)

40. Furthermore, *the findings of the current study can be used to decide* what kinds of strategies need to be included in the text books of each proficiency level in institutes to *make learning optimal.* (RA2)

41. *Implications from the study and concrete teaching strategies* aiming at facilitating Auditory implicit memory *are also suggested.* (RA8)

42. Social theories of decision making have long been concerned with understanding the less rational aspects of organizing, and *discourse studies of decision making would benefit from orienting to* such nuanced perspective. (RA3)

43. Only time will tell *whether we have committed hubris and over- reached or whether we have in fact identified some interesting new directions* that planning researcher could usefully explore. In so doing, we hope to contribute to the development of a radically new, and above all, 21st-century version of SLA studies. (RA8)

44. As the research agenda in LESSLLA context continues to evolve, *activity theory can serve as a useful, accessible tool for* researcher and teachers exploring classroom practice. (RA1)

From the examples above the author sells the findings of the study by explaining their contribution to the area being studied. Example 40 says the findings *'can be used to decide'* on new changes in textbooks. The researcher also explains the strengths and weaknesses in the methodology used so that future research studies could benefit from the strong points and avoid or improve on the weaknesses as can be seen in example 43 which states that *'only time will tell…'*

DM 6: Deduction from the research

Yang and Allison, (2003) say this move aims to enable the author to infer to the results, to suggest how to solve the problems and also identify gaps encountered by the study. It does this by pointing out areas for future study or by drawing pedagogical implications and significance of the present study by indicating the necessity for pedagogic changes. It is expressed using present simple tense and modal verb as well as statements relating to application of the results to learning and teaching contexts (Yang and Allison, 2003; Noudoshan, 2012) as can be deduced from the examples below:

45. Much *more research is needed in the domain of* linguistic L3/Ln acquisition of morphs morphosyntax. (RA10)

46. We therefore, look forward to collaborating with our connectionist and other cognitive colleagues in SLA on how these alternative meanings of emergence ultimately converge. (RA8)

47. ...and *discourse studies of decision making would benefit* from orienting to such nuanced perspectives. (RA3)

Example 45 is seen identifying a gap for further study by stating that *'more research is needed'* and example 47 mentions the pedagogical significance of the findings of the study in RA3 by saying that there is a *'benefit'* to be had in the area of study from the results presented by the study.

DM6 (Deduction from the study) comes as a follow up of DM5 (Evaluating the study). DM5 mentions the contribution of the current study and points out the strengths and weaknesses and DM6 uses these weaknesses to point out future areas for study as seen in the data extract examples above.

DM6 is a concluding move. It brings the discussion section to a closure by relating the findings of the study to the field of study. In some cases where the RA does not have a conclusion section then this move also serves to sum up the whole research work.

Therefore, such findings would be in agreement with previous studies on Discussion section (see McKinlay, 1984; Swales and Feak, 1994; Holmes, 1995, and 1997; Rasmeenin, 2006; Yang and Allison, 2003). All these studies report that Move 3 (commenting on results) is the most prominent move followed by Move 2(Summarizing Results) in the Discussion section of a RA.

Earlier studies though proposing different number of moves (Yang and Allison, 2003; 7-move model; Hopkins and Dudley-Evans, 1988 – 11-move model; Swales, 1990 – 8-moves model) all agree that commenting on results is an obligatory move in this section. This argument is supported by the fact that this move had the highest frequency of occurrence as compared to the rest of the moves found in this section.

Literature reviewed also agrees that the communicative focus of this section is to comment on the findings of the study thus the section title; Discussions- meaning to discuss/ comment on the findings. I therefore ascertain that in order to comment on results then a statement(s) on the results accompany the comments. The statement of results in the Discussion section is mostly a summarized form of the results presented in the Results section. This translates to DM2 (Summarizing Results) and DM3 (Commenting on Results) being the most frequent moves in the Discussion section of a RA and DM3 (Commenting on Results) being the most frequent move hence mirroring the rhetorical function of the Discussion section – to discuss results in the RA.

Comparing the Rhetorical Structure of the Results and Discussions sections

I objectively propose here that there are similarities and differences in the rhetorical structure of the Results and

Discussion sections of the RA. For purposes of comparison I juxtaposed the rhetorical move structures of the Results and Discussion sections and the frequency of occurrence of each move. This enables the researchers to see at a glance the general appearance in terms of rhetorical moves of both sections.

I also affirm that there are both similarities and differences in terms of move occurrence and move structure of the Results and Discussion sections in RAs in Applied Linguistics. First, it would be observed that each of the two sections has six rhetorical moves as shown in Table 4.3 below:

Table: Rhetorical Structure of Results and Discussion Sections

Moves	Elements	Results		Discussion	
		Freq. (n)	%	Freq.(n)	%
Move 1	(R)Preparatory Information/ Background Information	41	2.9	14	1.0
Move 2	(R) Reporting Results/(D) Summarizing Results	566	40.4	53	3.8
Move 3	Commenting on Results	238	17.0	263	18.8
Move 4	(R) Summarizing Results/(D) Summarizing the Study	132	9.4	31	2.2

Move 5	Evaluating the study	12	0.9	29	2.1
Move 6	Deductions from the study	7	0.5	16	1.1
	TOTAL	996	71.0	406	29.0

N= 1402

To determine the percentage, the formula used is n/N × 100

Where each item e.g. RM1 = n

The aggregate frequency (total moves in both Results and Discussion sections) = N

Percentage = n/N × 100

Secondly, in regard to move occurrence it is noted that there is a similarity in the frequency of occurrence of the obligatory moves. In both sections Moves 2 and 3 are the most dominant with Move 2(Reporting results) taking the highest frequency (40.4%) and Move 3(Commenting on results) taking the second position (16.8%) in the Results section and the two moves interchanging positions of dominance in the Discussion section: Move 3(Commenting on results) took18.8% and Move 2 (Summarizing results) has 3.8%.

This interchange in dominance is attributed to the difference in communicative focus of each section since the Results section's main communicative purpose is to report findings of the study whereas the Discussion section aims to discuss the findings of the study, (Yang and Allison,

2003; Rasmeenin, 2006; Nodoushan, 2012). Thus Move 2 (Reporting results) dominates the results sections while Move 3 (Commenting on results) is dominant in the Discussion sections.

This difference in the use of moves as noted in this corpus could also be attributed to what Lewin et al (2001) and Yang and Allison (2003) reported. They state that using moves in different sections of Applied Linguistic RAs is restricted by time and space, similar previous research, subsequent sections in the RAs; the writer's being a novice or an esteemed veteran member of the discourse community, and writer's personal judgment to express the amount of information in order to convince the audience.

It can, therefore, be concluded that omitting of some of the moves and their recycling in the results and discussion sections of RAs as seen in here (Tables 4.2 and 4.3) are the results of the factors outlined above.

Also, both sections (Results and Discussion) seem to agree mostly on how they label the moves: for example move 3 in both sections is seen to comment on the results of the study, move 6 gives deductions from the study after move 5 of both sections has evaluated the study. All these moves (in Results & Discussion) need to be introduced to the reader by use of move 1.

From the ongoing reports it can be seen that the two sections proceed to report and comment on results and then summarize either the section (in the case of Results section) or the study (in the case of Discussion section) and end by evaluating the study and by giving deductions from the study. Although, the labels are the same, the moves are realized and signaled differently in the sections as discussed in the individual sections.

Although, Move 5 (Evaluating the study) and Move 6 (Deductions from the study) in both sections are similar, these last two moves are quite infrequent in the Results section (0.9% and 0.5% respectively) but features more in the Discussion section (2.2% and 2.1% respectively). This high frequency of occurrence of Moves 5 and 6 in the Discussion section may be that the author may want to create an awareness of the importance of his/her study. This is in order to attract attention to the RA by outlining the importance of the present study and providing practical implications for pedagogy in the area of study as well as make suggestions to encourage other writers to conduct more research in the field of study.

It should also be noted that there is no linear move structure (M1-M2-M3-M4-M5-M6) appearing in either of the sections under study. The reason is that the moves are cyclical thus the lack of a linear move-structure. The differences in terms of the order in which moves are presented in the texts could be an indicator that the preferred order depends on the writer's preference for dealing with the information collected in the study (Lewin et al, 2001 and Yang and Allison, 2003).

The moves are highly cyclical with one or more moves being repeated and especially Move 2 (Reporting results in the Results section and Summarizing results in the Discussion section) and Move 3 (Commenting on results in both sections) in both sections studied. The cyclical pattern of moves is prevalent in both Results and Discussion sections of Applied Linguistics RAs. This supports the findings by

Peng (1987), Dudley-Evans (1988), Swales (1990), and Holmes (1997). These researchers reported that moves in the RA in different disciplines appeared in cyclical patterns in terms of their sequencing.

It is affirmed here that the only moves that are highly cyclical are M2 (Reporting results in Results sections and Summarizing results in Discussion sections) and M3 (Commenting on results in both Results and Discussion sections). The only difference is on the frequency of occurrence in each section. In the Results section the move structure has Move 2 occurring at a higher frequency than Move 3 and in the Discussion section, Move 3 took dominance over Move 2. This is attributed to the main communicative focus of each section since the Results section's communicative focus is to report results whereas the Discussion section's communicative focus is to discuss the findings of the study.

The high cyclical occurrence of moves in the RAs may be due to the fact that the RD sections are where the author presents his/her point(s) based on the findings of the study. The author has greater freedom to generate ideas (present and comment on results as well as conclude the study) which are relevant to the specific study (Swales, 2004). This freedom may account for the differences in frequency and cyclical nature in the order of moves in these sections.

Most Results and Discussion sections are presented cyclically with Move 2 (Presenting results) in the Results section and Move 3 (Commenting on results) in the Discussion sections being the most cyclical – Move 2 is the most dominant and cyclical in the Results section and Move

3 being the most dominant and cyclical in the Discussion section in our corpus.

The move that takes dominance in terms of frequency and being more cyclical appears to be determined by the communicative focus of the RA section- Presenting results in the Results section and Commenting (discussing) on results in the Discussion section. This is as far as the referred study could deduce from the analysis but there ought to be room for further research to explore more possible reasons for the differences noted.

Summary

This chapter reports and discusses the findings of the study in line with the objectives of the study. For example, in this section it is reported that the sections studied were found to have a six-move rhetorical structure with some elements in the structure overlapping in both sections studied but with a difference noted in terms of the rhetorical functions served by each section.

CHAPTER FIVE

Summarizing Findings, Conclusion and Recommendations

Introduction

In this chapter, I bring together all the ideas on the rhetorical structure of the Results and Discussion sections of the RA in Applied Linguistics as per the findings of the study guided research questions. After tying the findings together, I also give conclusions based on the study's findings and lastly outline pedagogical implications of the study and make recommendations on areas for further research in genre analysis of RAs.

Summary of Findings

The analysis here is of the RA published in well-established journals in Applied Linguistics with the following questions as a guideline:

1. What are the rhetorical structures of the Results and the Discussionsections?
2. What are the rhetorical functions of the Results and the Discussion sections?
3. What similarities and differences exist between the rhetorical structures of the Results and Discussion sections?

I have found and reported that the Results/Findings section was obligatory in a RA in Applied Linguistics. This is because this section occurred in all the RAs in the corpus. This is to say that this section is mandatory for a RA to be seen as complete. This is because every study must present its findings. Even when a section title is topic-specific rather than generic it is still found to be presenting results - the communicative focus of this section. Every researcher sets out to research some hypothesis and must therefore, report what they found out, therefore, the requirement to have the Results section.

I have also found and reported that a RA must also dedicate some section to discuss the results presented. It is found that all the RAs in the corpus featured a section on Discussion – whether as a section on its own or occurring together with either Results or with Conclusions thus; Results and Discussions, 1 RA; Discussions 6 RAS; Discussions and Conclusions, 1 RA. This gives a total of eight RAs with an explicit section dedicated to discussing results. Even where a RA lacked a section titled Discussion the study still finds it to have a paragraph(s) discussing the results presented. A RA is also found to have the Conclusion section as obligatory and that this section summarizes the study and gives practical pedagogical implications as well as identified gaps for further research in the field under study.

I have identified a six-move framework for the RA Results section and some of these moves are also found to serve more than one purpose that helps in realizing the communicative function of the move at a more specific level. For example, a move such as Discussion Move 5 (Evaluating the study) has several functions: mentions contribution of the study to the field, highlights the limitations of the findings of the study as well as point out the strengths and weaknesses of the methodology. All these helps to realize the communicative function labeled Discussion Move 5.

I have also identified the most dominant and the obligatory moves in this section. Move 2 (Reporting results) is found to be the dominant move in the Results section thus shaping this section's communicative focus as that of reporting results. Move 2 (Reporting results) and Move 3 (Commenting on results) are the most integral moves in the Results section as they have the highest percentage of occurrence (57% and 24% respectively).

The Discussion section has a six-move structure as in this analysis and has Move 3 (Commenting on results) as the most dominant move with 65% frequency and Move 2 (Summarizing results) as the second most dominant move with 13% frequency. This section's communicative focus is to discuss results.

The moves in the two sections are found to be quite cyclical in nature. It emerges that Move 2 (Reporting results in the Results section and summarizing results in the Discussion) and Move 3 (Commenting on Results in both sections) has a high cyclicity tendency in both sections studied and the remaining moves take lesser frequency and are less cyclical.

The findings agree with previous studies on these sections of a RA in Applied Linguistics on the communicative focus of each section as well as on the idea of the moves being cyclical (Peng, 1987; Dudley-Evans, 1988; Swales, 1990; and Holmes, 1997). These researchers reported that moves in the RA in different disciplines appeared in cyclical patterns in terms of their sequencing. The cyclical pattern of moves is common in both Results and Discussion sections of Applied Linguistics RAs.

On the type and number of moves in the Results section of the study agrees with the literature reviewed (Yang and Allison, 2003). In the Discussions sections have identified a six-move scheme although I was using Yang and Allison's (2003) seven-move scheme as its guideline. I found their Move 2 (Reporting results) and Move 3 (Summarizing results) to be referring to the same function and so I conflated the two moves to become my Move 2 (reporting results – whether in full or summarized version). I also found that the Discussion section just summarized the results that had already been reported in the Results section and did not give the results move much space as I did the move on commenting on results.

To answer the third question the findings report identifying both similarities and differences in terms of move occurrence and move structure of both sections studied. In both sections Moves 2 and 3 (Reporting results in the Results section and Summarizing results in the Discussion) and Move 3 (Commenting on Results in both sections) are key to ensuring that the section is complete and that it communicates what it is intended to do – report results (Results section) and discussing results (Discussion section).

The difference is in terms of the most dominant move in terms of frequency of occurrence: Move 2 (Reporting results) is dominant in the Results sections and Move 3 (Commenting on results) take the highest frequency in the Discussions section as earlier discussed. Move 4 (Summarizing the results in Results section and Summarizing the study in the Discussion section) in both sections also does the same function of summarizing the work – either summarizing the results hence Results Move 4 or summarizing the study – Discussion Move 4.

In terms of Move Structure, I have noted that there is no linear Move-structure (M1-M2-M3-M4-M5-M6) in either of the sections studied. The lack of a linear move structure is attributed to the cyclicity of the moves in the sections studied. There are instances of most moves recurring and especially Moves 2 and 3 in both sections studied. The cyclical nature of the moves in these sections is attributed to the freedom accorded a researcher to present and comment on the findings of his/her study.

From my findings, it emerges that there are elements commonly found between the two sections in terms of the types of moves and the communicative functions of the moves and that they are cyclical in nature as well as having differences in terms of the most dominant move in each section which shapes the communicative purpose of each section.

Conclusions

From my findings I have concluded that the titles and section headings a writer gives to his/her sections give some idea of the role s/he sees the section playing or in telling the reader what the author hopes to accomplish in a given section. This role determines the moves to employ in each section thus determining the communicative purpose of each section which then determines the section's rhetorical move structure.

It is also noted that there are overlapping elements between the results and conclusion sections in terms of the type of moves and communicative functions as well as areas of difference in terms of what move is dominant. The findings agree with previous studies (Holmes, 1997; Yang and Allison, 2003; and Kanokslapatham, 2005) in terms of the communicative focus and the most dominant moves and the cyclical nature of the RD sections of the RA in Applied Linguistics. I noted that the results section focuses on reporting the findings of the study while the discussion section comments on the results presented. This focus, then determines what moves are obligatory and more frequent in the two sections. Move 2 (reporting results) is found to be more frequent in the results section while Move 3 (commenting on results) is the dominant move in the discussion section of the RA in Applied Linguistics.

The findings also show that there are well-established conventions within the discourse community of Applied Linguistics RA writing as regards the way researchers have to make the results of their investigations known. This is because, in spite of the small corpus of our study, the findings have prove to be of close similarity with those reported in earlier studies in the field (Thompson, 1993; Brett 1994; Williams, 1999; Holmes, 1997, 2007; Peacock, 2003; Yang and Allison, 2003; Holmes 2007, Nodoushan, 2012).

I therefore, conclude that the Results and Discussion sections of the RA in Applied Linguistics move from presenting results through discussing them to summarizing the study. This is to say that the Results and Discussion sections of the RA perform three main functions: that of reporting results, that of commenting on results and that of summarizing the study.

RECOMMENDATIONS

Pedagogic Implications

From the findings, a few pedagogical implications in regard to the designing of teaching programs and materials can be drawn. Holmes (1997) observes that the phenomenon of inadequate materials and incomprehensive syllabi is very common. He further reports that this is due to the lack of awareness by curriculum developers to recognize the role of genre in academic discourse.

I have therefore outlined a framework for designing and developing syllabi and materials for classes on writing in the field of Applied Linguistics in both undergraduate and postgraduate studies. It is worth noting that it is important to familiarize learners with the genres in their disciplines as this improves their comprehension of both written and spoken discourse in their respective discipline. The acquired knowledge also makes the learners more effective, efficient, creative and flexible and thus confident in written and spoken discourse for increased participation in their discourse communities. According to Mahmood and Simin (2010) there is need to familiarize students with genres of RAs so as to enable them to look at RAs not as texts but as a way of the authors interacting socially with other members in their discourse community.

Due to the increased number of graduate students, I therefore, suggest that instructors of academic writing be aware of the standard rhetorical move structure of the Results and Discussion subgenre of the RA and to emphasize to their students to observe the standard move-structure for each subgenre in their academic write ups. These instructors should analyze RA Results and Discussion sections with their students in class and also give them a lot of practice work. This practice will make the learners move-sensitive and aware of the discourse community's expectations and so enable them to produce RAs that are acceptable as they bear the standard rhetorical move structure (Mahmood and Simin, 2010).

I am also of the view that pedagogically, integrating the RA genre in the curriculum would be a helpful idea for the teachers of English as a second language. For example, to gain competence in academic writing learners need to be informed of the expectations in their discourse community and they should be instructed to see the ordering of moves and the relationship that exists between the functions of the moves and the way language is used by the authors. It is my view that this will help learners and especially L2 learners who are required to write academic papers either for publication or a partial requirement for a given award, to generate effectively a paper that is acceptable in their discourse community.

Sheldon (2011) says that writers of a RA need to bear in mind the context of their work in relation to their audience and especially the discourse community to which they operate in. I therefore opine that RA writers need to be aware of and to display an understanding of the rhetorical move structure of this genre and particularly the Results and Discussion subgenres (they are not widely studied) which function to present and explain research findings to the readers, will enable upcoming writers to plan their written and spoken discourse in a form that leads to higher chances of acceptance in their discourse community.

Since it has been observed that there is need for a genre-base teaching approach in our curriculum, I recommend that the academic writing instructors be made aware of its importance in improving the quality of their students written and spoken discourse. This will make the students produce discourses that meet the conventions of the different discourse communities and thus more acceptable, communicative and interactive.

I also recommend that the curriculum developers have a curriculum that includes genre based studies in its syllabi and that adequate time for teaching the academic writing process is allocated. They should also develop adequate teaching-learning materials to ensure that the students get the required information and adequate practice both in dealing with the writing process and in analyzing the end product of this process. This will ensure that the learners are well prepared to join and to participate wholly, effectively and efficiently in their respective discourse communities.

Suggestions for further research

I have only analyzed the rhetorical move structure of Results and Discussion section of RAs in Applied Linguistics in internationally published journals. It is notable, thus, that there is room for more comparative studies on the rhetorical move structure of Results and Discussions in RAs produced by both native and non-native writers and published in both international and local contexts. It is also worth mentioning that few studies have been done in this area which still leaves room for more comparative studies. Research based on this suggestion will find out the factors that influence writers and so lead to the variations in rhetorical strategies that a particular writer adopts when writing in varied published levels and fields.

I have not investigated on factors such as personal choice, and other variables such as author's background, writing and publishing experiences. A study on this and particularly on interviewing the article writers would make such a study produce more reliable results because interviewing can enhance the understanding of the above-mentioned variables (Flowerdew & Wan (2010).

More studies should be done regarding RAs of different disciplines. This is because there is need to carry out genre analysis studies in different disciplines as well as comparative studies between disciplines. This will help inform the students on the similarities and differences that exist in different RAs depending on the discipline from which they originate. It seems that inter-disciplinary genre analysis studies are few and not conclusive on the rhetorical move structure of the Ras researched on.

It is also worthwhile to conduct a study that combines the RA as a finished product and the writing process –I have looked at the RA as a product. A study combining the two levels will provide knowledge to students on the process of creating a RA and the stages of development in-between to getting a finished RA and getting the same published. This will help students know how to deal with the different levels of writing a RA since it is noticeable that not many students ever get to write a publishable RA. Those that write publishable RAs also shy away from the rigorous process of getting the RAs published.

Genre analysts could also do a study of conference papers-the process of generating a conference paper and presenting the paper orally at a conference, what factors guide the authors to decide what to include and what not to include in their oral presentation. The writing of a conference paper involves two stages: writing and reading (Martin, 2013). A study could be done on the process of presenting the paper and how the author deals with presentation issues such as pacing, rhythm and vocabulary. One could also study how the author of a conference paper deals with the two processes: writing and reading.

Another understudied area involves the publishing of monographs. There is room to study the process of transforming a dissertation into a monograph. A comparative study could also look at the differences and similarities in content between a dissertation and a monograph.

Summary

In this part of the book, I summarized the results of a specific study and given the conclusions arrived at as well as identified the gaps in the study that could provide a basis for further study. This section concludes that the Results and Discussion sections have similar number of rhetorical moves only that the Results section has Move 2 as the dominant move while the Discussions section has Move 3 taking dominance. This dominance is in accordance with the Communicative focus of the different sections.

References

Atkinson, D. (2005). *Situated qualitative research and second language writing.* Mahwah, New Jersey: Lawrence Erlbaum Publishers.

Bazerman, C. (1988). *Shaping written knowledge: The genre and activity of the experimental article in science.* Madison: University of Wisconsin Press.

Beaugrande, R. (1985), "Text Linguistics in Discourse Studies" in T.A. Van Dijk (Ed.) (1985), *A Handbook of Discourse Analysis,* Volume 1 London, Academic Press.

Beaugrande, R. and Dressler, W. (1981), *Introduction to Text Linguistics*, London, Longman.

Beaugrande, R. and Dressler, W. (1985), "Text Linguistics in Discourse Studies" in T. A.Van Dijk (Ed.) (1985), *A Handbook of Discourse Analysis,* Volume 1 London,Academic Press.

Belanger, M. (1982).*A preliminary analysis of the structure of the discussion sections in ten Neuroscience journal article.* (Mimeo), LSU, Aston University.

Berkenkotter,C. and Huckin, T. (1993). Rethinking genre from a socio-cognitive perspective. *Written Communication, 10, 475-509*

Berkenkotter,C. and Huckin, T. (1995) *Genre Knowledge in Disciplinary Communication. L*awrence Erlbaum Associates.

Bhatia, V.K. (1993). *Analysisng Genre: Language use in professional settings.* London: Longman.

Bhatia, V.K. (1998). Generic conflicts in academic discourse. In Fortanet I., Posteguillo S., Palmer J.C. &Coll J.F. (Eds).*Genre studies in English for academic purposes (p15-28). Castello de la Plana:* Publications de al Universitat Jaume.

Bhatia V.K. (1999). Integrating products, processes, purposes and participants in professional writing. In Candlin C.N. and Hyland K. (Eds).*Writing texts, processes and practices.* London: Longman.

Bolivar, A. (1994). 'The Structure of Newspaper Editorials,' in R.M. Coulhard (Ed.), *Advances in Written Text Analysis* (London: Routledge): 276-294

Brett, P. (1994). A genre analysis of the result sections of sociology articles. *English for Specific Purposes,* pp. 47-56

Bruce, I. J. (2008a). *Academic writing and genre.* London: Continuum

Bruce, I. J. (2008b). Cognitive genre structures in methods sections of research articles. *English for Specific Purposes,*7(1), 39-54.

Bunton, D. (2005). The structure of PhD Conclusion Chapters, *Journal of English for Academic Purposes,* 4, 207-224.

Coe, R., Lingard L., &Telsenko T. (2002).*The Rhetoric and ideology genre,* USA: Hampton Press Inc.

Cohen, L., Manion, L., & Morrison, K. (2007).*Research Methods in Education.* New York: Routledge.

Conduit, A. & Modesto, D. (1990). An investigation of the generic structure of the materials/methods sections of scientific reports. *Australian Review of Applied Linguistics,* Series S, No. 6, 109-134.

Connole, H., Smith, B., & Wiseman, R. (1993).*Research Methodology 1: Issues and Methods in Research.* Victoria, Australia: Deakin University.

Connor, U. (1990). An investigation of the generic structure of the materials sections of Scientific reports. *Australian Review of Applied Linguistics,* Series S, No. 6, 109-134.

Connor, U. (1994), Contrastive rhetoric: *Cross-cultural aspects of second language writing. Cambridge University Press.*

Cooper, C. (1985). Aspects of article introduction in IEEE publications

Creswell, J. W. (2012). *Educational Research: Planning, Conducting and Evaluating Quantitative and Qualitative Research.*(2nd Edition). USA: Pearson Education, Inc.

Crookes, C. (1986). *Towards a validated analysis of scientific text structure. Applied Linguistics journal* 7:57-70.

Denzin, N., & Lincoln, Y. (2003). *Hand book of Qualitative Research.* (3rd Ed.). Thousand Oaks, CA: Sage.

Dudley-Evans, T. (1986). Genre Analysis: An investigation of the introduction and discussion sections of M. Sc. Dissertation. In M. Coulthard (Ed.), *Talking about text* (*Discourse Analysis Monographs No.13, English Language Research).* University if Birmingham.

Dudley-Evans, T. (1994). Genre analysis: an approach to text analysis for ESP. In Coulthard, M. (Ed.), *Advances in written text analysis.*(p. 219-228).London: Routledge, 219-228.

Dudley-Evans, T. (1999). The dissertation: A case of neglect? In P. Thompson (Ed.), *Issues in EAP writing research and instruction.* University of Reading: CALS. (pp. 28-36.)

Dudley-Evans, T. (2000). Genre analysis: A key to a theory of English for Specific Purposes. URL: www.uv.es.aelfe/wedRAs/RA 2 Dudley.pdf.

Duszak, A. (1997). *The Schematic Structure of literature Review in Research Articles of Applied Linguistics.* New York: Mouton de Gruyter.

Edmondson, W. J. (1981). *Spoken Discourse: A Model for Analysis.* London : Longman.

Flowerdew, J. (1999). Writing for scholarly publication in English: The case of Hong Kong. *Journal of Second Language Writing*, 8,123-146.

Flowerdew, J. (2000). Using a genre-based framework to teach organizational structure in academic writing. *English Teaching Journal* 54, 4,369-378.

Flowerdew, J. (2002). Genre in the Classroom: A Linguistic Approach. *Genre in the Classroom. Multiple Perspectives.* New Jersey: Lawrence Ealrbaum Associates.

Grabe, W. & Kaplan, R.B. (1996).*Theory & Practice of writing.* Longman.

Good, M. (2013). Publishing your First Journal Article: an Academic Publisher's View-1. Cambridge University press.

Gosden, H. (1993). Discourse functions of marked themes in scientific research articles. *English for Specific Purposes*, 11, 3,207-224.

Habibi, P. (2008). Genre Analysis of Research Article Introductions across ESP, Psycholinguistics and Sociolinguistics. *International Journal of Applied Linguistics, Vol. 11, No. 2, 87-111.*

Halliday, M. A. K. (1978). *Language as Social Semiotic: The Social Interpretation of Language and Meaning.* London: Edward Arnold.

Halliday, M. A. K., (1985). *An Introduction to Functional Grammar,* London: Edward Arnold Ltd.

Halliday, M. A. K., & Hasan R. (1976). *Cohesion in English.* London: Longman.

Halliday, M. A. K., & Hasan R. (1989).*Language, Context and Text: Aspects of Language in a social Semiotic Perspective* (Oxford: Oxford University Press, 2nd Ed.)

Hasan, R. (1989). The identity of a text. In Halliday M.A.K. & Hasan R. (Eds.) *Language, text and context* (pp 97-117). Oxford: Oxford University Press.

Hatch, E. (1992).*Discourse and Language Education.* Cambridge: Cambridge University Press.

Hewlett, C. (2002). How to publish your journal paper. *American Psychological Association Journal*, Vol. 33, No. 8, Pp. 50.

Hills, S. S., Soppelsa, B. F. & West, G. K. (1982). Teaching ESL students to read and write experimental research papers. *TESOL Quarterly, 16/3, 333-347.*

Holmes, R. (1995). Genre analysis and the social sciences: an investigation of the introductions, background sections and discussion sections of research articles in history, political science and sociology. *English for Specific Purposes*, 16, 3, 45-56.

Holmes, R. (1997). Genre analysis and the social sciences: An investigation of the structure of research articles discussion sections in three disciplines. *English for Specific Purposes,* 16, 4, 321-337.

Hopkins, A. (1985). An investigation into the organizing and organizational features of published conference papers. *English for Specific Purposes,* 5, 325-342.

Hopkins, A., & Dudley-Evans, T. (1988). A genre-based investigation of the discussion sections in articles and dissertations. *English for Specific Purposes*, 7, 113-122.

Hyland, K. (2004). *Genre and second language writing.* Ann Arbor, MI: University of Michigan Press.

Hyons, S. (1996). Genre in three traditions: Implications for ESL. *TESOL Quarterly*, 30(4), 693-722.

Jogthong, C. (2001). *Research article introduction in Thai: genre analysis of academic writing.* Unpublished PhD dissertation, West Virginia.

Johns, A. M. & Dudley-Evans, T. (1991). English for Specific Purposes: International in Scope, specific in Purpose. *TESOL Quarterly, 25, 297-314.*

Kanoksilapatham, B. (2005). Rhetorical structure of biochemistry research articles. *English for Specific,* 24, 269-292.

Kanoksilapatham, B. (2007). Rhetorical moves in biochemistry research articles. *Discourse on the move: Using corpus analysis to describe discourse structure. Studies in corpus linguistics* (Vol. 28, pp. 73-119. Amsterdam: John Benjamins.

Karanja, L. (1993). *"A Discourse Analysis of KBC TV Broadcast Discussion Programs."* Unpublished M.A. Thesis, University of Nairobi.

Lakic, I. (2010).*Analysing Genre: Research Article Introductions in Economics.* University of Montenego.

Lewin, B. et al. (2001). *Expository discourse: a genre-based approach to social science research texts.* Continuum. London

Lovejoy, K. B. (1991). Cohesion and Coherence in Text. *Linguistics and Education,* 4(3)1- 18.

Macken, M., M. Kalantzis, G. Kress, J. Martin, & J. Rothery. (1990). *A Genre-Based Approach to Teaching Writing,* Sydney: Directorate of Studies.

Maroko, G. M. (1999). *Rhetorical structure in Master of Arts (M.A.) research proposals of Kenyatta University.* Unpublished M.A. Thesis. Kenyatta University. Kenya.

Maroko, G. M. (2008). *A genre analysis of selected Masters of Arts (M.A.) and science (MSc.) thesis of Kenyan Public Universities.* Unpublished PhD Thesis. Kenyatta University. Kenya.

Maxwell, J. A. (1996). *Qualitative Research Design: An Interactive Approach.* California: Sage Publications.

McCloskey, D. (1986). *The Rhetoric of Economics.* Brighton: Wheatsheaf.

McKinlay, J. (1983). *An analysis of discussion sections in medical journal articles.* University of Birmingham, UK.

McKinlay, J. (1984). *An analysis of discussion sections in medical journal articles.* Unpublished M.A. dissertation, University of Birmingham, UK

McMillan, J. H., & Schumacher, S. (2001). *Research in Education. A Conceptual Introduction.* Fifth Edition. Boston: Addison Wesley Longman, Inc.

Merrian, S. (2009). *Qualitative Research: A Guide to Design and Implementation.* San Francisco, CA: Jossey Bass.

Miller, C.R. (1984). Genre as social action. *Quarterly Journal of Speech,* 70, 151-167.

Nelson, A. (2000). *A corpus-based study of the lexis of Business English and Business English teaching materials.* Unpublished PhD. thesis. University of Manchester: Manchester.

Nodoushan, M. A. S. (2012). A Structural Move Analysis of Discussion Sub-genre in Applied Linguistics. *International Journal of Language Studies,* http://www.ijls.net/.

Nyongesa, B. W. (2005). *Kenyan Newspaper Discourse: An Investigation of Rhetorical Structure in Editorials as Argumentation.* Unpublished M. A. Thesis, Kenyatta University.

Nwogu, K. (1997). The medical research paper: structures and functions. *English for Specific Purposes,* 16, 2: 119-138.

Ogutu, E. A., (1996). *'An Analysis of Cohesion and Coherence Structure in Texts Written by Secondary School ESL Learners in Kenya.'* Unpublished PhD Thesis. University of Birmingham.

Onguko, S. O. (1999). A Comparative Study of Cohesion in Academic and Newspaper Texts. Unpublished M.A Thesis. Kenyatta University.

Paltridge, B. (2001). Linguistic Research and EAP Pedagogy in J. Flowerdew, & M. Peacock (Eds.), *Research Perspectives on English for Academic Purposes (pp. 55-70);* Cambridge: CUP

Paltridge, B. (2002). Thesis and dissertation writing. An examination of published advice and actual practice. *English for Specific Purposes* 21: 125-143.

Peacock, M. (2002). Communicative moves in the discussion section of research articles. *System,* 30(4), pp. 479-497.

Peng, J. (1987). Organizational features in chemical engineering research articles. *EnglishLanguage Research Journal,* 1, 79-116.

Pojanapunya, P., & Todd, R.W. (2011). Relevance of findings in results to discussion sections in applied linguistics research. Proceedings of the International Conference: Doing research in Applied Linguistics. King Mongkut's University of technology Thonburi and Macquarie University.

Pollard, N. (2004). The Art of Getting Published. *Student Pulse: The International Student Journal,* 1, Northeastern University: Boston.

Posteguillo, S. (1999). The semantic structures of computer science research articles. *English for Specific Purposes,* 18, 2, 139-160.

Qin,Qiubai. (2000). Genre Analysis and Its Implications for EFL Teaching. Lecture notes of Summer School for foreign language teachers in China, Hangzhou, Zhejiang. *In US English Teaching*, 2, 11, 22-25.

Rasmeenin, C. (2006). *A Structural Move Analysis of MA Thesis Discussion Sections in Applied Linguistics.* Unpublished MA Thesis, Mahidol University.

Rymer, J. (1998). Scientific composing process: How eminent scientists write journal articles. In D. A. Jolliffe (Ed.), *Writing in academic disciplines.* (pp. 211-350). Norwood, N.J. Ablex.

Salager-Meyer, F. (1990). Discoursal flows in medical Engineering abstracts: a genre analysis per research- and text-type. *English for Specific Purposes 6,* 365-385.

Salager-Meyer, F. (1992). A Text-type and Move Analysis Study of Verb Tense and Modality Distribution in Medical English Abstracts. *English for Specific Purposes,* 11(2), 93-113.

Samraj, B. (2002). Introduction in research articles: variations across disciplines. *English for Specific Purposes,* 13, 2, 28-42.

Silverman, D. (2005). *Doing Qualitative Research: A Practical Handbook. (*2nd Edition). London: SAGE Publications.

Sinclair, J. M. (1986). 'Fictional worlds.' In M. Coulthard (Ed.): Talking about text. Birmingham: University of Birmingham ELR.

Snape, D., & Spencer, L. (2003). *Qualitative Research Practice: A Guide for Social Science Students and Researchers.* New Delhi: SAGE Publications, London, Thousand Oaks.

Stubbs, M. (1995). 'Grammar, text, and ideology: Computer-assisted Methods in the Linguistics of Representation.' Applied Linguistics 15/2:201-23.

Swales, J. (1981). Aspects of article introduction. Birmingham, UK: University of Aston Language Studies Unit.

Swales, J. (1990). Genre analysis: English in academic and research settings. Cambridge, U.K.: Cambridge University Press.

Swales, J. (2004). Research genres: Exploration and applications. Cambridge: Cambridge University Press.

Swales, J. & Feak, C. B. (1994). *Academic writing for Graduate Students: Essential Tasks and Skills,* Ann Arbor, MI: The University of Michigan Press.

Swales, J. & Feak, C. B. (2003). *English in Today's Research World: A Writing guide,* Ann Arbor, MI: The University of Michigan Press.

Swales, J. & Feak, C. B. (2004). Academic writing for graduate students: Essential tasks and skills (2nd Ed.). Ann Arbor: University of Michigan Press.

Taylor, G., & Chen, T. (1991). Linguistic cultural and sub-cultural issues in contrastive discourse analysis: Anglo-American and Chinese texts. *Applied Linguistics,* 3, 319- 336.

Taylor, G., & Francis C. (2008). *Genre analysis from the Linguistics Encyclopedia,* 2nd Ed. Bookrags, Inc.

Thompson, D. (1993). Arguing for experimental "facts" in science: a study of research articles sections in biochemistry. *Written Communication*, 10, 106-128.

Walsham, G. (1993). *Interpreting Information Systems in Organizations.* Chichester, NH: Wiley.

Waseema, T. (2006).How to End an Introduction in a Computer Science Article. A Corpus- based Approach, *Language and Computers,* 60 (1) 227-241.

Waseema, T. (2010). Literary Texts in the Language Classroom: A Study of Teachers' and Students' Views at International School I Bangkok, *The Asian EFL Journal* 4(12) 173-213.

Weissberg, R. & Buker, S. (1990). *Writing up Research.* London: Prentice-Hall International (UK) Limited.

Widdowson, H. G. (1978). *Teaching Language as Communication.* London: Oxford University Press.

Widdowson, H. G. (1996). *Linguistics.* Oxford University Press, USA.

Williams, I. (1999). Results sections of medical research articles: analysis of rhetorical categories for pedagogical purposes. *English for Specific Purposes,* 18: 347-366.

Wirada, A. & Wannaruk, A. (2013). Investigating Move Structure of English Applied Linguistics Research Article Discussions Published in International & Thai Journals, *English Language and Teaching, Vol. 6. No. 2*

Wood, A. S. (1982). An Examination of the Rhetorical Structures of Authentic Chemistry Texts. *Applied Linguistics* 3: 121-143.

Yang, R. & Allison, D. (2003). Research Articles in Applied Linguistics: Moving from results to conclusions. English for Specific Purposes, 22(4), 365-384.

Yang, R. & Allison, D. 2004). Research articles in applied linguistics: structures from a functional perspectives. *English for Specific Purposes, 22: 365-380.*

Yang, R., & Edwards, C. (1995). Problems and solutions for trainee teachers reading academic articles in English. In M.L. Tickoo (Ed.), Reading and writing: theory into practices (Anthology series 35) (pp. 366-382), Singapore Regional Language Centre.

Yin, R. K. (2011). *Qualitative Research from Start to Finish.* New York: Guilford Press.

Appendices

APPENDIX I

Journals used in the Sample Data in this Study

1. Journal of Applied Language Studies (Apples), Vol. 7, 1, 2013
2. Journal of Applied Linguistics and Professional Practice (JALPP), Vol.7, 3, 2013
3. International Journal of Applied Linguistics and English Literature, (IJALEL) Vol. 2, 2013
4. Modern Journal of Applied Linguistics, (MJAL), Vol. 5, 2013
5. Language Learning Journal, (LLJ), 2013
6. Journal of ELT and Applied Linguistics, (JELTAL), Vol. 1, 2, 2013
7. The Language Learning Journal, (TLLJ), 2013
8. Annual Review of Applied Linguistics, (ARAL), Vol. 33, 2013
9. Studies in Second Language Acquisition, (SSLA), 2013
10. International Journal of Applied Linguistics, (IJAL), 2013

APPENDIX II

Titles of RAs used in The Study, their Authors and the Journals Extracted From

1. 1. Farrelly R. (2013). Converging Perspectives in the LESLLA Context. *Journal of Applied Language Studies (Apples),* Vol. 7, 1, 2013, 25–44

2. Halvorsen K. (2013). Team decision making in the workplace: A systematic review of discourse analytic studies. Journal of Applied Linguistics and Professional Practice, (Jalpp) vol. 7.3 2013; 273–296.

3. Jafari S. & Kafipour R. (2013). An Investigation of Vocabulary Learning Strategies by Iranian EFL Students in Different Proficiency Levels. *International Journal of Applied Linguistics & English Literature (Online). Vol. 2; 24-28; November 2013.* Australian International Academic Centre, Australia.

4. Jiang F. & Yongbing L. (2013). Auditory Implicit Memory and Context Effect in Early EFL Learners. *MJAL5:3, pp. 143-162.* Spring, 2013.

5. Markee, N. and Kunitz, S. (2013), Doing Planning and Task Performance in Second Language Acquisition: An Ethno methodological Respecification. Language Learning, 63: 629-664.

6. Olaoye A. A. (2013). Nigerian Dress Culture: A Linguistic and Anthropological Communication Tool. Journal of ELT and Applied Linguistics (JELTAL) Volume 1- Issue 2, pp. 32-42, October, 2013.

7. Pauwels A. (2011) Future directions for the learning of languages in universities: challenges and opportunities, *The Language Learning Journal, 39:2, 247-257.*

8. Rothman J. & Halloran B. (2013). Formal Linguistic Approaches to L3/Ln Acquisition: A Focus on Morphosyntactic Transfer in Adult Multilingualism, *Annual Review of Applied Linguistics Volume 33, pp 51-67,* Cambridge University Press.

9. Rothman J. & Iverson M. (2013). ISLANDS AND OBJECTS IN L2 SPANISH: *Do You Know the Learners Who Drop____? Studies in Second Language Acquisition, 2013, **35**, 589 – 618.*

10. 10. Stelma, J., Fay, R. and Zhou, X. (2013), Developing intentionality and researching multilingually: An ecological and methodological perspective. *International Journal of Applied Linguistics, 23: 300-315.*

Printed in the United States
By Bookmasters